Be Unique
Be You
& Live!

David A. George

Acknowledgements

MANY THANKS!!!!

For me to be where I am, there are so many people and things in my life for which I am thankful. Quite frankly, I do not know where I would be without these people and things. Of course, to list everyone and everything would be a very impractical task without a doubt. However, I must acknowledge a few. Therefore, I wish to acknowledge the rest of all persons and things within groups and classifications.

I wish many thanks to my family and relatives who have supported me through the years. Some supported me economically and others nurtured me emotionally. All of these significant providers gave me a wealth of support and I very well could be lost without it. I want to thank all of the neighbors, counselors (tutors and camp), and school friends that I had between the ages of 5 and 9. Next to my Bethany College years, those were the happiest days of my life. Having a happy childhood during those years of innocence has made me a wealthy soul.

During my downward spiral between the ages of 10 and 18, I often felt very lonely, unappreciated, and unloved. I had severe periodic bouts of depression, which festered into a profound chronic depression during high school. However, I did have my music to keep me alive and humming along. It was a coping mechanism that kept my future dreams alive. I only had a few real, true friends during this period, which was dreadfully cold and brutal. Those few are still my friends today. Cheers to music and my two friends.

I owe a debt of gratitude to Bethany College, which, not only changed my life for the better but also actually saved my life. I must acknowledge Mrs. Chris Sampson who facilitated my admission into the Special Advising program at Bethany. She and all my professors helped me believe in myself and do well. I thank all of the brothers of Sigma Nu, who were very much like brothers to me. They were a part of the ultimate highlight of my life on the night of April 10, 1989 (see conclusion). I also must thank all of the girls that I was friends with. They were very much like sisters to me. In conclusion, I thank all of my friends, teachers and counselors who have guided me, and the Lord Jesus Christ. Many thanks!

Dedication

This book is for all individuals who are soul searching. Searching for what and who they need, where they need to be, and who they are. This book also goes out to everyone who is trying to learn more about themselves and be open to ideas that will inspire them to not only be inquisitive and continue learning, but also to grow into the most inspirationally unique individuals they can be.

To all individuals everywhere, who feel unknown, unwanted, unloved, denied, slighted, left out, and written off. Never throw in the towel. Continue to duke it out one round at a time in every boxing match that you fight in your life. Miraculously, you will be the golden gloves champion, again, again, and again. When you win the fight of maintaining your individuality, you can then declare victory in your own personal boxing ring, which will make you the prince or princess of pugilism. Never hang up the gloves and give up!

Introduction

Through the years, I suffered from a profound case of post-traumatic stress disorder, as well as chronic depression and a generalized anxiety disorder. All of these disorders are derived from having an extremely profound comprehension problem, which is essentially a learning disability, which has always forced me to work harder than anyone, including children who are much younger than I am.

I eventually sought help from a professional therapist. Some of my relatives and many of my friends commended me on doing so and expressed their love and care for me and their acceptance of who I am and what I am. I continued to unveil personal issues to my friends that I was ashamed to disclose before. I felt increasingly liberated.

What helped me even more was that I was getting reacquainted with special friends in Florida and other places before I moved back to Bethany. All of these individuals love me very much. This of course, made me more determined than ever to complete the book that you are holding in your hands at this moment. This book is a practical resource composed of autobiographical accounts and educational concepts based on research, experiences, and some very deep personal cogitation.

This literary entity stems from an individual with an innate, incorrigible problem who challenges you to get inside his mind to help understand that we are all only human. Everyone is unique and special. Our unique and special needs must be tended to. However, some people can't change certain things about themselves, especially if they were born that way through God. Nevertheless, this book should help you realize that everyone has personal strengths and talents, and these should be emphasized more than anything else.

If you are tired of feeling trapped, restricted, and denied the right to make your life extraordinarily unique, this just might help you formulate your own blueprint of how you can break free from those chains. This is your life and no one else's. Own it and live it!!

CHAPTER ONE

The Barrier Inside My Head

I know how it feels growing up with a condition that forces you to work harder than anyone you may ever know in your life. I was born with a profound learning disability that is totally with me to this day. I have a profound comprehension problem that is derived from some kind of central nervous system disorder that affects my brain. I don't know the etiology of the disorder. It will probably always remain a mystery. At any rate, it obstructs me from doing the most simplistic things as well as the most complicated things. This blockage or barrier inside my head (if you will) affects everything I do and it seems like it is a Catch 22, no matter what.

A childhood doctor of mine said that my brain is good, but there may be a few wires that are crossed, or there may be some blockage that hinders everything and slows me down.

Due to my condition being so profound and bizarrely rare, there may not be any formal diagnosis for what my condition is. Nevertheless, I still have something in my head that is innate; therefore, I can't change it. The difference is, I am older, wiser, and better equipped to face it and deal with it. I am conscientious about it in order to appear reasonably competent in social and professional situations.

Attention-deficit-disorder is derived from this neurological blockage. I was diagnosed with attention deficit hyperactive disorder as a little boy and I was believed to have a so-called learning disability. I was very hyperactive when I was little. I am still easily distracted now, as I was when I was a little boy. I was on Ritalin for some period of time. It was assessed by some specialists that my agitated behavior was predisposed through unpredictable and various situations. Yet my behavior was often rectified through intervention strategies. Of course, at a young age, it is not easy for a child to understand a condition of my caliber, let alone, know how to handle it. I have been off Ritalin for many years and I have become a very quiet, reserved person in many ways.

However, my condition is still with me and it will remain with me the rest of my life. I could always read and spell well. I could and can memorize and process some words and meaningful concepts that are color-fully and discretely picturesque.

I can name all 43 of the presidents in a row and name and recite all of the Super Bowl scores, the teams who played, and the MVP's of the first 20 Super Bowls. I have a great rote memory when it comes to memorizing certain pieces of information. I can visualize all 50 of the United States and memorize the capital names. You know how pictur-esque they are.

I can retain concepts, ideas, and basic information that I visualize. I can also have them modified through unique auditory sounds, especially music that authentically stimulates me in a powerful way, and the more any colorful image or segment of music conveys any artistic integrity or excitement, the more it stays tattooed in my brain, so to speak.

I can retain the meanings of words when used in a song or a movie or if they are said by any prominent figure. I can demonstrate things that I know by putting my knowledge into action, without being able to ver-bally explain it unless I can explain basics in a way that the listener can understand.

Of course, no matter how well I can relate to something, that would not guarantee doing well on tests and any other tasks that require a substantial amount of comprehension. I can remember concise details and I can recall things that have a linear sequential order to them.

More often so, I cannot absorb nonlinear, unpredictable things that come up spontaneously. I cannot even assimilate what I would have just read or listened to with the exception of merely remembering a few words. It doesn't matter whether they are books, paragraphs, or even brief sentences. In order for me to retain a sentence or maybe just a few words in a sentence, I would have to think of some colorful image of a person, color, song, or anything so distinctly memorable, just to retain a few words. Of course, I would only maintain it on a short-term level; I could easily forget it in a matter of minutes or seconds.

Even when I read to myself out loud, I must exercise enough mental and physical energy to concentrate reading one word at a time without stumbling or mispronouncing anything.

I do not absorb nor retain anything. It would take me constant, very, very long hours and many days to prepare for one test and speech, along with other things. Whenever I read something and I say to myself, "con-centrate on reading word for word and sound articulate," I do not as-similate most if any of what I have just read.

Sometimes when I read or hear something, it may remind me of something that will help me understand and retain the concept for a matter of seconds. However, my fixation on that component that is stimulating me, hampers me from comprehending anything else that I would continue reading or listening to.

I can become so fixated on one word, concept, or image, that I can only apprehend basic elements rather than comprehend multiple words or concepts, unless I spend enormous amounts of time preparing certain things that I need to know and understand.

I can excel in areas when I am able to focus on one element at a time through a straightforward, linear progression or structure. I would have to obsessively think about one particularly minute point that I hear or read by visualizing a particular person or thing that may be relative to whatever the subject is.

When I watch sporting events, I can follow one little play at a time, but I will not and cannot remember the previous plays; therefore, I miss so many other things going on because I am zeroing in on one little thing at a time. If questioned about them, I would not be able to say what happened. At the end of each game, I would only know the score, recall and restate some very distinct impressive plays, and that would be all. I would inevitably forget it all in a very short amount of time. Other than that, I would miss everything said or taught. This applies the same way when I read or try to listen to what is being said. I am barely able to remember just a few words that may be totally disconnected.

Sometimes I have to watch movies over and over again to get the gist of the dialogues. One minute element that I become focused on, like the way someone looks or a particular word or concept that is said, is so stimulating, that I am only able to retain it through relating it to something else that interests me. However, it could be totally unconnected to the main gist of the subject or motifs that are being explained in the dialogues that I am listening to.

Even when I am walking down the street, driving, happy and excited, confused, nervous, or sad and depressed, my condition is always with me. I can merely be the best I can be regardless of any modifications. Even when I focus on appearing attentive, just so I would not be suspected of daydreaming, I am still not absorbing or comprehending anything.

It seemed like I was in my own little world when I was very little because of my condition. My parents suspected that I may have had a hearing problem since I was not very responsive when they would call out for me.

Quite often, though, I was teased for supposedly daydreaming because I had ADHD. Sometimes I did pay attention well but I was easily distracted. Believe me, the students laughed at me and I was perceived as deviant. There was snide laughter and remarks made by my peers.

I was often accused of daydreaming. Even now my mind can wander no matter what I am doing, only I have mature ways of dealing with it.

I have trouble following directions but it's not necessarily that I do not listen. I actually do try to listen; I am just not able to assimilate anything because of some congenital element inside me that affects my brain, coordination, and my nervous system.

I have proven that I can do well, but I have to work very long on the most seemingly simple things in order to perform competently enough. For the longest time, I had to learn how to listen and to simply learn how to learn some of the most simplistic things. These would consist of learning how to tie my shoes, make my bed, fold my pants on a hanger properly, and a whole host of other things. I have overcome some of these obstacles but there are still some that I struggle with to this day.

I have accomplished some things that would seem like simple, remote stepping stones to some people, but they are milestones for me.

Almost everything I do that seems a little bit challenging takes an enormous amount of physical and mental energy, along with the endless amount of time to get it right. Even to light a candle or a match takes massive physical energy for me to do so, and people can see how shaky I am. I know that I have trouble holding things together sometimes because of some innate deficit in my central nervous system, which we know the brain is part of.

My penmanship has always been below par. It would often be sloppy when I vigorously wrote in cursive. I could read my own writing, but many others had trouble reading it.

There were times when engaging in sports that I would appear inept, even though I proved to be competent many other times. Ice hockey was always a sport that I was good at because I could concentrate and I was able to establish some composure and poise. I also learned how to skate very well, which enhanced my ability to play hockey.

I could run the ball and tackle someone well when I played football. When I played baseball, I consistently hit the ball well and I was able to get on base, but I was always sheepish about playing in the field because my condition hindered my coordination. I was able to catch fly balls, but it took an enormous amount of concentration and energy to do so, and I did not look very graceful. Basically, I could hold it together, but that was the best I could do. I just was not really dynamic because my physical coordination was, and still is, severely stifled.

Whether I am immensely tense or not, I can easily fall apart; however it may depend on the situations. I had the hardest time following instructions in physical education classes and other recreational functions. There were times when I looked pathetic and incompetent in the eyes of others. The same went when I was first learning how to play ice hockey. I was very angry because I knew that in some way, I was smart, but there were times when I was being judged as being strange, inferior, and of course, stupid.

I knew that there was something that made me feel inadequate, but I didn't understand what it was and I was just trying to be human. I have had to study well over 10 times harder than anyone, just studying and practicing seemingly simplistic and complex things. I take notes diligently and I read them over and over again to prepare and perform efficiently. No matter what, anything else that is said or anything that I read would invariably and dreadfully suffer, unless I was given the opportunity and time to prepare. Even now, I have to write myself notes or verbally say things to myself when I am told to do something after I have at least tried to listen to what someone has said.

The only way I would be able to comprehend things was by obsessively and compulsively spending enormous amounts of time, repetitiously preparing for specific tests and quizes through any sort of mental and vocal rehearsal. This would include recitals of speeches or lectures, and every minute of the day counted in order for me to prepare. I would relax and try to socialize within intervals. There were times when I could not commit myself to any social excursions because I had to work within such tight structural constraints. I had to really isolate myself from others to concentrate, absorb material, and prepare enough, so I could at least do marginally well, even though I did produce first rate results other times.

In my classes, I would concentrate on taking voluminous notes so I wouldn't miss anything the lecturer would say, but it was no use in trying to comprehend most of what was being said. Then I would have to compulsively go back to studying and assimilating everything, which took a colossal amount of time. I had to mentally shut off anyone and everything that surrounded me. I still have to do that to this day. If I relax my mind for any short duration, I don't assimilate anything.

I realized that I had to read everything step by step, without trying to absorb too much, too soon, because I was, and I am still, not able to do that anyway. Every second of every day counted for me. I could read twenty pages of a book one night, and then, I would have to spend maybe two hours, just trying to absorb that in itself. Even if I understood it well enough, and was prepared for a quiz the next day, I would have to spend at least two or more additional hours on a combination of homework assignments that were ruthlessly bombarded on me, and with which I had a terribly difficult time to begin with. I wouldn't be able to tend to the other assignments, especially if they were very difficult, which just about everything was for me, no matter what.

It was and still is hard to balance everything out that I do in my life. If I worked hard on one thing, and I had done well as a result, other study priorities would falter, though that was not so much the case for speeches and research papers.

I sometimes didn't turn in classroom assignments during one period in my life either out of fear of ridicule if I did badly or I just said to hell with it, because I just wanted to be a kid and have fun by playing with the others. I was made fun of based on my daydreaming problem. The teachers seldom did much to deter that. I would continue to struggle to follow directions.

I was scared to ask for help because I would get screamed at for incomplete assignments, relying on others too much to help me, and of course I feared receiving very poor grades. I was accused of not listening, daydreaming, being in a daze, and so forth. It is not that I can't understand meaningful concepts, because I actually can but there is some kind of innate neurological deficit that I have that hinders me and sometimes even keeps me from absorbing and retaining anything that I am supposed to learn.

Being physically and mentally impulsive are believed to be universal characteristics of someone diagnosed with ADD. I certainly have those traits. I used to fidget a great deal, and part of the reason why I did, was to help conjure up ideas or to simply think. Everyone else perceived them as idiosyncratic habits, which they may have been in some ways, but they actually helped me in many ways. Nobody even tried to understand that.

My fidgeting habits were becoming more obvious and many people, including teachers and my so-called friends, made a sport of ridiculing me in academic and social situations. This really substantiated my inferiority complex. People seemed to think that any aberration that I had invariably constituted a stigma. I am mentally impulsive in a way which I may instantly think of one idea so quickly, I forget what I may have done or thought in the mere seconds that follow.

Whenever I appeared unwilling to help in remote, mechanical situations that I was very slow in learning how to do or simply could not do, I was accused of being self-centered and inconsiderate. I was accused of being lazy, selfish, apathetic, and anything else that generated self-defeating thoughts. People accused me of making excuses. That was not the case at all. I was terribly misunderstood.

What made it worse was the fact that I had grown up in an area comprised of persons who were ruthlessly authoritative, explosively temperamental, extremely impatient, belittling, and viciously critical. These persons had no understanding of my problem. They were so cold and not the least bit empathic. I was always blamed and belittled when something would go wrong. I can recall statements such as "can't you do anything right"; "you always make a mess"; "whenever something goes wrong or something breaks, you're usually the one who is responsible"; "you don't listen"; "get your head out of the sand," and the like.

I became a scapegoat. I had fallen prey of what is called victimizing the victim. They all told me that I didn't pay attention. The real problem was that no one paid attention to my problem.

I was often very frustrated, bitter, jealous, and hateful that I had to work harder than anyone. It seemed that I was not entitled to have some fun, and enjoy life with others.

I was a happy child during the years that I was 5, 6, 7, 8, and 9. I had the power and resources to imagine and dream. I had actually done well in school during this period in my life. I could simply be myself through the means of cooperation, before I was forced to compete with anyone.

I did not always have the compassion and understanding that I could have used then. However, I did have plenty of resources, such as a family with a good financial status, playtime/recreation, a safe neighborhood to play in with neighborhood kids, and the opportunity to acquire a solid education.

My academic and social problems in school did not start to dramatically ensue until a month or so after the second semester of my 4th grade year. I could begin to feel the barriers in my life taking greater precedence than the resources. Math was becoming more difficult for me, and so were other things that demanded substantial comprehension. My self-esteem was very low for many years, and I was often perceived as lazy and/or stupid, and I was made to feel like a loser or a second-class citizen. I often learned things through being humiliated. I guess that was the only good thing about learning the hard way and I learned it more than ever shortly after I began the 6th grade.

CHAPTER TWO

A Fish Out of Water

I attended an all-male prep school starting from the 6th Grade, through my senior year. I should have known for sure by the end of 7th grade, that the school I attended was not fit for me, and it was only going to get terribly worse in the next five years. I have to admit that I did like the school in some ways when I was in the 6th and 7th grade.

However, the competitive mentality of this school encouraged teachers and students to taunt and castigate the students with weaknesses. There was little appreciation, not to mention respect, for students who were creative, practical thinkers like myself. I was interested in engaging in other activities that made me feel useful, creative, and alive.

I was forced to do nothing but study with no interaction in extracurricular activities. I had to tend to multiple homework assignments and massive quantities of information to study for quizzes and tests, which would most often intertwine together. Believe it or not, some assignments would be completed at best (but were poorly done) or I would barely pass quizzes or tests on certain days and do fairly well, at best, on other assignments. Nevertheless, I would inevitably bomb everything else terribly.

There were many homework assignments that I struggled with, and there were tests that I had difficulty preparing for. I sometimes blew them off partly because I had other things to do that would take more time. I also wanted to engage in other events, just so I could at least get some adequate rest and relaxation.

I began to think more and more about creative things that I liked to do that were deviant from the curriculum. Furthermore, I was depressed just knowing that I was in an area that forced me to do nothing but study and learn, which I had difficulty to begin with. I was so resentful that I concentrated on thinking creatively and practically to make myself feel intelligent.

There were times when I became lazy, not just because people indoctrinated me with that, but I also did not want to acknowledge that I had a problem to be reckoned with, just so I would not look so pathetic in the eyes of others. I didn't know how to balance everything out, simply because I could not. Not only was I angry and defiant about how I needed to work when I sometimes didn't have the appropriate tools to succeed, but I was intimidated about getting help, because I was often vehemently chastised or made to feel inferior.

I was often accused of lying when I thought that I understood something, and I was not able to explain it well. I was also accused of not studying at all nor preparing when I actually did try. I had to tend to so many other things and very little would get done. People would get frustrated with me by showing a lack of compassion, empathy, and understanding. I was viciously belittled and insulted by people, let alone terribly mortified. Part of the problems that I had were that I still needed to learn how to learn through unusual, colorful learning strategies that some of my teachers did not have the background nor the training to teach me.

There were frequent times, then and now, when I will try to listen to what people say in personal conversations or lectures and I would be able to recite something back sounding like a human tape recorder. I would not always sound like I fully comprehended what I just said. Science and Math were particularly difficult in this respect when I had taken tests.

There were times when I understood basic concepts when I was getting extra-help, especially when I was able to remember things through visualization and repetition. But whenever I encountered components that looked different or unusual to me, my condition sparked me to overanalyze the most remote inklings in ways which I would think to myself: "What if This" or "How Come There Is This," and I would bomb several tests or assignments as a result. I would have to spend countless hours studying over the specifics and even some of the basics in order to articulate them substantially.

One of my high school history teachers suspected me of cheating on his tests because he didn't think that I could perform well enough on a B level based on my history grades from the previous years. You see, he didn't even bother to consider any underlying factors, such as an individual's learning style and ability, which was profoundly deviant. He said that he was not trying to tear me down or discourage me, but he was concerned about consistency, since my grades were on a general and consistently low level at this prep school.

Even when I produced some first rate results on tests, speeches, or anything else during this era of my life, I was still contrasted with other students who made the honor roll and the ones who excelled in sports. Those qualities were demanded to meet the elite (ahem) standards of this so-called prestigious institution, whose main objective was collective power over individual empowerment. I was subjected to a narrow world of oppressive competition that seemed more significant than compassion, cooperation, and empathy.

There was massive emphasis on the allocation of deficiency reports to students. These generated stigmas that were horribly humiliating to the students, especially when the reports were made available to all of the faculty and wrongly accessible to the entire student body.

People at this school were so hung up on looking and feeling powerful rather than realistically conceding that an individual's uniqueness must be enriched no matter what type of learner the student was. I think the constrictive environment that I was in impeded my morale to be assertive, and since I did not want to feel like a misfit, I tried to make believe that my condition did not exist.

One thing that parents, teachers, and others fail to acknowledge is that kids, especially teenagers, think in the present moment. They want to live in the here and now and have a good time. I was like everybody else in that respect. I was trying to be human, creative, and happy which was not easy for me to do. I was determined to blend in with my peers. It seemed to me, that the more that I would study, the more that I would be grimly reminded that I had a profound problem that I was made to feel ashamed of at a very young age. I remember the first semester of my 7th grade year, of how I tried so hard and I did well part of the time, but I was alienated from others socially.

So during the second semester, I tried to be more sociable, so I could blend in and be more cultivated. My grades suffered of course, but I became more compatible with my peers by expressing my personality at times, and being a conformist because I feared being rejected.

That does not mean that I was never remiss about anything nor always so innocent. There were times when I had done some naughty things that I am not proud of. I was sometimes vindictive against others who picked on me, to prevent being subjugated by the general consensus of persons who appeared to be powerful. One person said, "You are what your friends are." Sadly, that is true in many respects. No one wants to feel cast out, which is natural and understandable. However, that is no excuse for any actions that I am guilty of.

My conscience caught up with me telling me that I am a beautiful person on the inside and that I must become that rather than becoming something that could transform me into a monster. I learned to be very empathic of others. Much of those ideas came from conceding my personal weaknesses and knowing that I am very sensitive.

I did have some friends who I acknowledged later, as so-called friends.

The relations and interactions with these people were very superficial.

I learned at a young age that real friends were hard to find, and from that era, I only had maybe 2 with whom I am friends today.

My peers would try to play pranks on me, because they thought that I was too naïve and stupid, to see that they were scheming something. There were a few teachers of mine who did the same. On the whole, they could see that I was not fooled, but they kept trying anyway. Eventually, it came down to my peers trying to find new ways of teasing me as if to say: "If we can't find one way to mess with him, we shall find another."

There were often times when these two-faced, back-stabbing buddies of mine would try to expose my weaknesses anyway they could by vehemently putting me down, calling me names, insulting me and patronizing me in a way to make it sound that they were only kidding. Even if they didn't mean any terribly hard feelings, they were not just joking. They probably did it as a means to defend themselves, in case they got in trouble, then they would claim that they were only kidding to evade any potentially severe punishment.

It was not fair to be told that I could not have some fun and to not concentrate on things that make me feel creative, intelligent, and special, even if those qualities seemed like anomalies to our societal school system. What really angered me was that I repressed talents and abilities that I did not know that I had. Sure, academics come first, but that does not mean that any academic setting is proper for just anyone and everyone.

In spite of the grief that I suffered during my prep school years, I dreaded the idea of attending a public school, partly because I did not know many people. My parents feared that I would have had a harder time being admitted into any colleges if I had transferred. Although I suspected that I would have done better academically, I feared being picked on and ostracized if my peers detected any of my learning weaknesses. Then I would be continually rejected and taunted by them.

I felt spiritually and intellectually impoverished in many ways, since I was stuck in the middle of two cruel worlds. I became defiant and resentful of education, because I was embroiled in a setting where I should not have been in the first place: A FISH OUT OF WATER!!!!

In retrospect, if I could change the past, I would have attended an exclusive school perhaps in the New England area, designed for academically challenged yet creative and practical students. I would have started it in the 8th grade.

The curriculum would have been structured in a way, which I would take no more than four classes a semester. It would be like a college curriculum. There would be study sessions designed in a cooperative, nurturing setting, which the teachers and tutors would acknowledge the students' unique weaknesses and strengths.

The school would have had a sports program, along with extracurricular activities, such as intramurals. It would have been like taking science, math, music, or physical education the first semester, and having the option of taking at least one creative class once during the entire school year, even though the classes would be different each semester. Basically, I would have wanted an extensive liberal arts education that would have allowed me to work at my own pace, but I would have had to earn it.

I was displaced and I was trapped in something inappropriate that lacked resources that would have been vital to me. I needed to be some place where I belonged, just like a fish belongs in water. I was a fish out of water.

The homogenized mainstream in which I lived did not incline me to think objectively or critically. This was not just because I feared ridicule, but also because I sensed that I would end up feeling more shame for asserting myself about my legitimately complex inborn problem and people would laugh at me. I was still uncertain of my problem during my teen years. I was more self-conscious about being ridiculed when I was a teenager, so I did whatever I could to prevent any major derision.

I had several harrowing experiences at the prep school that I attended. One experience regarded one of my English teachers from high school. He was sympathetic to me in a very belittling way. He would ruthlessly call on me in class to answer questions from reading assignments that I had only a limited time to prepare for.

Furthermore, I was bulldozed into a dimension that some might call "factory schooling," during which students are thrown into a giant manufacturing machine and the components (the students) are required to be transformed into entities that comply with the shallow, rigid, conventional standards that are ruthlessly imposed on them; courtesy of our cultural norms.

I had to assert myself against a number of persons who were shallow, egotistical, dictatorial, callous, arrogant, and mentally abusive. It was a no-win situation for me. Some of the worst things about it were that I felt so suppressed expressing my feelings or who I really was because I was often being contrasted with others who did so much better. I did not want to acknowledge my weaknesses because I feared that I would set myself up for more derision and ostracism. That of course, would champion an even more profound inferiority complex.

I don't consider myself to be a talented person. I have always been lousy at art. My condition obstructs me from being even remotely adequate in many ways such as drawing pictures of people and things. I am simply incompetent when it comes to artistic talent (drawing).

I had one teacher who would often chastise me by saying how I didn't follow instructions, or he would tell me to get busy and don't talk because I could not afford to like the others. He had no idea what was wrong with me, but he humiliated me in class by saying "You do nothing in my class"; "You just might fail this grading period." He had no clue as to what my problem was and he tried to make me feel ashamed of it.

It seemed to me, the general consensus was that I had to study hard all of the time whether my social and emotional needs were met or not. "If you are not happy, that is too bad!! Study, produce, and be happy!"

It almost seemed like I did not have the right to be happy or to conversely feel sorry for myself when I needed to. Some would have said "get over it man, and quit being unhappy and sullen." "If we want your opinion, we will simply give it to you." I was told to study hard, get good grades, and buckle down.

I was taught to accept the norms and deal with them. "If you don't like it, too bad! You must have an attitude problem, therefore, you should be at a public or catholic school because you won't learn anything at those schools anyway." That's what they wanted us to believe so we could be part of the cozy monarchy that they were nestled in. They seemed to think the rest of the world orbited around their shallow little world.

All of the students at this prep school were made to think that if we did not stay at this school, we would not do well in college, and we would be disadvantaged for the rest of our lives. I must admit that I was taken by this indoctrination. I never really questioned those ideologies at a young age, because competitive, shallow concepts were bestowed upon me when I was little, and I was profoundly sheltered in some ways. I guess I vegetated in a mainstream social structure that I never had anything to compare to or contrast with until I attended college.

Subconsciously, I could feel a spiritual hollowness pervading through me, but I did not fully realize it until much later. I was supposed to think and behave like a robot, not necessarily to produce all A's and letter in every sport, but I was told that I must hit the books all of the time, which meant I could not take the time to think about music and girls because I could not afford to. Does that make sense? Does that seem fair or reasonable? Of course it doesn't!! That is very dehumanizing!! I am a human being. A living organism of flesh and blood! I had a right to want to feel happy and have a life. It is not that I did not want to work hard and do well, because I did. I just wanted to be in an environment that was appropriate for me.

Even when I was sad, anxious, and depressed, my disability was with me and it would stifle me even more to be productive, especially when my results were not compliant with the shallow, uncompromising institutionalized standards that were enforced upon me.

I had to dwell in a cruel, totalitarian academic setting, composed of students and many teachers who were superficial, two-faced, hypocritical, and arrogant. There were many teachers at the school who I thought were absolutely incompetent.

There was gossip about me being the student who had a zero on a Geometry test, which I was not. I remember one of my false friends nominating me for a class officer position to make everyone laugh. Many of my false friends and peers that I was forced to deal with were mocking and taunting me in utterly childish ways well into their senior year. Some had grown up to a degree, but many remained very immature. I was antagonized and badgered by people in many ways. For example, students would taunt me by saying the names of certain girls that I liked whenever I was present.

There was a massive amount of mental and emotional abuse inflicted on me. If I made any little mistakes inside or outside of school, I would be criticized and analyzed in a condescending and demeaning manner. I was even scandalized through bad rumors composed of half-truths, innuendoes, and blatant lies. Many rumors were sparked by my so-called friends (back-stabbers & hypocrites).

I always tried to be as genuine as I could be. In some ways, it paid off, but I did pay a price for being a sensitive maverick during my teen years. I became very estranged from people, since I only had a few really true friends who hung out with others whom I did not get along with at all.

I was often very depressed and miserable. I was also beginning to think about girls more than ever, which got in the way of other school assignments and anything else that I had done. It was like I was not allowed to think of anything else outside of school. I wasn't supposed to think about girls either. Since I had little, if any, emotional support to begin with from people, it became all the more painful for me to bear. I basically became a zombie; I was alive and dead at the same time. I would often crawl into a cave to cope with my pain. In order to do so, I had to shut everyone and everything off.

There were days when I would sit or lay in my room and compulsively weep because I felt so futile, lonely, empty, and unloved. I was also devoured with remorse for not standing my ground firmly enough with people. I knew that very few, if any, would back me up. That is probably why I was afraid to assert myself. That partly explains why I felt so much emptiness.

I felt like such an unknown. I had to painstakingly knock myself out, just to get people to know me. I had to do so at the expense of making a fool out of myself. It was hard for me to meet people in places when I couldn't see them any other time, since I attended a different school, which had no girls. People were in their own cliques. I was trying to figure out, completely on my own, who I was without any compassionate input from anyone else.

The isolation and loneliness that I endured was very painful and depressing. I was so miserable to begin with, because I often suffered from severe periodic bouts of depression. Eventually, the depression was chronic and profound. The depression undermined not only my academic performance but also doing the most simplistic things outside of school. My depression also adversely affected my physical energy because my morale was so low. There were times when I was able to function efficiently enough academically, but I became such a mountain of anxiety, I would forget to preserve certain parts of my physical hygiene. My depression exacerbated that dimension even more. I showered and everything, but there were times when I neglected other aspects.

I was severely depressed in high school due to the lack of loving friendliness and affection from girls, since I was in an all-boys school and the small number of girls I had known were from other schools. I would seldom ever see girls. I felt that I needed some friendly, loving affection from them. I did not think it was unreasonable to have one friendly conversation on the phone with at least one girl a week. Others seemed to disagree. Some girls that I was friendly with had betrayed me, and they did not care to even give me the compassion and understanding that I really needed.

People didn't seem to care enough about whether I suffered from depression or not. I wasn't getting any counseling or psychological help. I was told to think about school and absolutely nothing else at all times, which would discredit any notions of seeking counseling or therapy.

People, especially the ones that I was seemingly close to, were not compassionate nor empathic in understanding that my emotional investment in music gave me a reason to live. It also may have helped me prevent a disaster such as vindictively harming others who put me down, attempting suicide, or self-destructing through some terrible mental breakdown that could have put me on a psychiatric ward. Most of this would have come from being a fish out of water.

I only ended up having a few dates in high school, including my senior prom. I wouldn't have thought it would be so hard; but it was and I really tried desperately. Feeling like such a stranger, who was marginally accepted by some, it was hard to meet people in order to develop healthy relationships unless I was cultivated into a socially and spiritually enriched realm, which was what I needed. I really began to feel despondent during the early part of my senior year in high school.

Finding a date for the Homecoming dance saved me from doing something drastic. I toughed it out for the rest of my senior year which wasn't easy. My so-called friends were more disrespectful to me than any other time that I had attended the school.

I thought about girls and women all of the time. I would fantasize about cultivating deep, interpersonal friendships and having dates with some of them. Eventually, I was able to achieve those things once I attended college.

However, my world was so profoundly deprived of those things when I was in Jr. high and high school. I had just a few dates over a period of four high school years.

Needless to say, I have had a very tough time in my life. My condition can slow me down in ways that may make me appear pathetically inept, too anxiety prone, lazy, apathetic, uncoordinated, extremely tense, lacking confidence, spaced out, or even mentally retarded.

On the other hand, I have been very fortunate in many ways. I had the economic resources that provided me with quality food, clothing, and shelter. I had my happy memories of my childhood before the age of 10. I also had dreams of making better, truer friendships than the ones that I had at the time.

I come from a family that is very financially well off. My relatives and ancestors worked very hard to earn the money that they had made. My father had worked especially hard and honestly not just for me but for all of us. He always enjoyed his work and he did not feel that I was a burden.

When I was a senior in high school, I was evaluated as to whether I had a learning disability or not. A specialist at a mental health agency determined that I had a disability of some sort and he did acknowledge whatever anxiety I had. However, he realized that I did very well on the qualitative testing, and he understood that I bombed the quantitative parts (puzzles and the like).

He was actually concerned that he would not be able to convince prospective college admissions and special advising programs that I had a learning disability because of my high qualitative scores. My overall grade point average was low and my SAT and ACT scores were terribly low.

Two colleges rejected me and one college required me to take a preliminary course before the school year would begin. If I did not pass the course, I would not be accepted into that college. Come July 1988, one very special college accepted me, and my life started to change for the better and forever.

CHAPTER THREE

Saved at Last!!

I entered Bethany College as a freshman in the fall of 1988. I was in a Special Advising Program with other students who had similar experiences to mine, but most of them did not have to work as hard as I had. At any rate, I was finally in an environment that provided the resources and tools in order for me to succeed.

My Special Advising instructor at Bethany became a mentor for me, and bless her heart, she instilled a light in my eyes that was never there before. She helped me understand that I was intelligent, regardless of my condition. She and other professors, fellow students, and friends encouraged me to accept myself and be true to myself for what and who I am. Though I may have to compromise and sacrifice more than many others, I could still lead a fruitful academic and social life in college and beyond. My professors, friends, and peers thought I was intelligent too.

They also taught me to accept failure any time when I failed some tests, and there were actually some that I did fail. There were even some classes that I had earned some C's in. On the whole, I did very well earning some A's and B's during the four-year period.

I worked hard and I finally earned the compassion, understanding, and respect that I deserved. I always knew that I was smart, cool, and special in my own way, and I deserved the chance to prove it. I earned a 3.25 GPA at the end of my first semester of my freshman year.

I pledged a fraternity, which helped me make the best friends that I ever had in my life, along with ones that I made outside of it. I had several dates over a period of four years, even though I never had time for a steady girlfriend, and many of my friends had several more dates than I had. I needed to establish friendships with numerous girls as though they could be sisters of mine, the same way with my numerous Sigma Nu fellows who were like brothers to me, because I had extremely little of the sort before. I was truly loved and cared for by both brothers and sisters.

Bethany was, and is, a diverse, cooperative environment that bolstered my inclination to be honest, assertive, and open to others and with myself. I was finally in a world where I was able to behave congruently with who and what I am.

I graduated from Bethany with a Bachelor's Degree in Communications in 1992, with an overall GPA in the B range. I was very proud of that and so was my family and all of my friends. I went on to work in radio for two years and then I aspired to seek a Master's degree in Counseling, since I was always interested in Psychology. I came close to earning the degree with a 3.8 GPA but then I realized that I needed to work in a setting that required structure because of my condition. I have been doing so for some time now. My condition is legitimate. It would and has been more obvious in more mechanical situations and anything that would take an enormous amount of deep analytical thinking.

I have been told by several people over the last sixteen years that they thought that I was bright. They said that they would never have guessed that I had such a profound problem, based on the way that I communicate with my articulation skills. That is all part of my point. I have strengths to be reckoned with, and I have created ideas to develop those strengths.

From my time at Bethany and through the years, I had overcome my difficulties by learning how to learn. I was able to do this through relating ideas to things that interested me such as the meaningful words and ideas in the song lyrics in the music that I love and any poetry that I might have read. All of these things helped me absorb and remember things on a long-term level as opposed to short-term. I was able to comprehend and retain ideas and meanings through listening to the words in the dialogues in the movies and television programs that I would watch. I was able to do this more if the subjects in the movies had anything to do with sports, murder mysteries, crime dramas, romance or anything that I could relate to my personal experiences in life while interacting with fellow human beings. That was another problem. I was trapped in an utterly pathetic, constrictive world that stymied me from having a life where I could engage with others in a number of different settings. I was socially competent as anyone else and no more naïve than anyone else my age, except about some of the terribly shady things that some of my peers were involved with (using and dealing drugs, extreme vandalism, theft, drinking on the school campus).

I was finally put to the test in the laboratory of experience by doing things in the community and being involved with a number of people on a social level while working on any projects that were academically or professionally oriented. This not only enabled me to retain the interesting meanings of any words that stimulated me through the years, but I was essentially able to relate basic and specific ideas in so many particular areas to other areas. For example, I finally retained the meaning of the word "enzyme" by relating the meaning of the word "catalyst" through how a music performer said how playing a central role in a story became an outstanding catalyst for him because his character role changed him as a powerful individual figure. The musical may have made a change in him but it did not dramatically change the musical itself (Giuliano 90).

What helped me the most was realistically acknowledging that education is meant to be something inspirational and personally enriching and since I love music so much, I was able to relate my love of music to a love of learning. When the meanings of words are modified through music (social, political, psychological, and philosophical issues), not only do I absorb things easier, I am more inclined to learn other things about life. What we are dealing with in every dimension of education is life and life is meant to be inspirational, right? After all, music is a source of inspiration for everyone. Every time I struggle to comprehend something, I remind myself that learning is meant to lift me up the same way music and lyrics lift me up. This does not change my difficulties in a way that they vanish, it just helps me put everything in perspective by knowing that I have overcome obstacles and I will continue doing so.

I still have to comprehend a multitude of things to do well and I cannot do so at the same exact pace of many others. Nevertheless, I have overcome my difficulties in a way where I know that I am capable of learning and doing well because I finally have been taught to learn how to learn by relating ideas and concepts from one thing to things that personally interest me. My specific interests come from my unique personality. Keeping this in mind, you should all be inspired to believe that you have the abilities and skills to do well. Moreover, you should be blessed with the wisdom to know that you have the power to succeed in school and life. If I am able to do it, you can definitely do it!!

I had come to the realization that if I was entitled to the same empathy and respect that I earned over the past sixteen years, why was it not granted to me while I was growing up? Why should anyone have to go through such horrific mental abuse and dehumanization? Now sure, we all have our faults and we all make mistakes, but we all need to be confronted with them in a constructive way rather than ways that are destructive. Everyone is in need of that.

I know that some people are naturally impatient and some people are set in their ways, but I have learned more than ever over the last seven years, that thoughts affect the way that we feel. If we are taught how to put things in perspective without being overly catastrophic, we become wise, empathic, and understanding. This concept helps to open the mind which helps open the heart. This interchangeable process helps everyone realize that everyone is unique, not to mention human.

Therefore, I wish to teach the importance of keeping an open mind for not only persons with learning disabilities but persons and creatures from all walks of life. I want to teach the importance of cooperating with others, and to concede that every individual is unique, and he or she must have the unique resources to succeed, and no one can do it alone.

More than that, being unique consists of having weaknesses, and if some are born to be academically, mechanically, and occupationally challenged like me, we should concede these weaknesses as realistic factors and approach them with compassion, understanding, empathy, and mercy. I was seldom approached with these elements.

Several of these factors, along with other ones, have compelled me to implement my writing endeavor. I think my condition and God's plan for me have blessed me with my ideas, and they have substantiated my mission in life.

I wish to underscore my condition as a reality, rather than a tragedy, so I can generate hope and inspiration for the entire human race. My plan is not to formulate nor teach any specific learning strategies and workshops that enable one to do better in school nor the workplace. My mission is to create and generate theories and concepts to help you understand that you are unique, and to inspire you to open your minds to life. I am hoping that I will be able to bless others with the wisdom to develop and implement specific ideas, tools, and resources that will help us flourish, as well-educated unique individuals.

I think God has created me to challenge others to be more perceptive and aware that we have strengths and weaknesses. This includes the entire human race. I think that if I have the opportunity to exercise my endeavor, I will give others the courage and humility to break free from the barriers that have been imposed on them. This can be done by enabling others to open their minds and hearts to all aspects of life.

My harrowing experiences could have been worse. Keeping that in mind, I am indeed grateful that I have survived. Nevertheless, nobody should have to experience the victimization that I had gone through. Therefore, I am challenging all of you to think very carefully about what I have imparted to you and do not take it for granted.

Most importantly, I wish to stress that it is not unreasonably selfish to have your emotional needs met in order to succeed in life and be happy. It does not make you inferior or wimpy at all. It makes you stronger because it makes you more human. If you stand tall as a unique individual to love and embrace others for what and who they are, you will be more inclined to teach our children those principles. They are our future.

We all need love, compassion, understanding, empathy, and the economic resources to succeed in life. If I did not have any of those things, I don't know where I would be today. Unlike myself, there are others who have been denied those privileges. Some end up on welfare, homeless, destitute, in prison, or dead. We all need to work hard and be willing to compromise. We also need to be willing to accept ourselves and accept whatever mistakes and failures we make. That's how we learn most everything anyway.

We must cooperate with each individual before you compete in this world. We all need more resources than barriers, just like we need more models than we need critics. We all need that "Chicken Soup For The Soul" (book), so to speak. That soup can be made up of love, affection, and having others acknowledge and embrace that special part of you that creates a spark that burns inside you. You all must follow that spark to change your life for the better and to help others positively change their lives. You start this process by accepting yourself for who and what you are and simply being yourself: The Unique Individual.

Basically I was not accepted for who and what I was. I was forced to not accept failure and mistakes and to see them as taboo. All of this comes from ignorance. Don't allow yourselves and the ones that you love to be defeated by this. Ignorance has notoriously proven how it has the potential to destroy the lives of others. We simply cannot let ignorance prevail.

CHAPTER FOUR

Ignorance

Ignorance is defined as "knowing little or nothing; without knowledge; caused by or showing a lack of knowledge; uninformed; unaware" (Thorndike and Barnhart 504).

"Prejudice is defined as a preconceived judgment or opinion without just grounds or sufficient knowledge" (Axelson 155). Maintaining prejudiced thoughts can lead to unethical actions toward unique persons inside or outside of groups based on superficial characteristics (155).

Groups that are victimized by prejudice are often distinguished by race, geographic areas that they live in, ethnicity, religious denominations, socioeconomic class, gender, age, national origin, and disability status (physical, mental, learning, and the like). Prejudice is derived from ignorance, which spawns bigotry, racism, bias, discrimination, and stereotyping.

One's humanity should be the primary part of each person, especially if all individuals are given the opportunity to demonstrate it, which they well deserve.

I do not believe in maintaining homogenized conventional standards that do not help a person grow as an individual. Many persons often repress their talents without ever knowing they actually have them when they are blocked from being themselves. These rigid standards are often derived from ignorance. There are numerous elements that come from ignorance. Some of these are shallowness, prejudice, arrogance, hypocrisy, hate, oppression, vandalism, and mayhem. These have adverse reciprocating effects on others. That is a tragedy for any human being and nobody deserves it.

The bottom line seems to be that we must concede biases against specific groups of individuals, before remedying anything that is wrong. (Martin and Osborne 344-45). Damaging labels, whether they are derived from racial bigotry, disability, national origin, political opinions, the government that you live in, religion, age, and gender can spawn stereotyping and discrimination, which are part of prejudice. Prejudice is derived from ignorance.

I was labeled as being dumb, stupid, retarded, and anything else the same way persons of different races are disparaged with racial slurs, labels, and stereotypes.

A stereotype is "an oversimplified generalization about the character-istics of members of a group" (Martin and Osborne 342). Many people, especially minorities, fall prey of these. Stereotypes are misconceptions because they perceive the members of the stereotyped group to have the same characteristics.

There may be remote elements of truth with some stereotypes that are basic and limited, but what is more credible are the distinct individu-als within the groups rather than how much they may be alike (343).

Native American Indians have been stereotypically depicted as fierce, uncivilized barbarians in the movies and on the tube. Thankfully, how-ever, <u>Dances With Wolves</u>, the Oscar winning film with Kevin Costner, conveys more humanistic and civilized depictions of Indians (Martin and Osborne 345). Keeping this in mind, it is important to see persons as unique human beings with distinct individualities and it is not fair to feel overpowered by a majority group of people who pretentiously claim to see people as individuals.

I have learned from my past experiences, especially with my learning disability, that when one doesn't fit the mold, he/she may feel overpow-ered by the general superiority of others. Persons with superiority com-plexes are determined to fulfill their supposed needs for power at the expense of persons with so-called inferiority complexes. Persons who manifest such bold self-assurance on the surface are more insecure than we really know. They are consumed with the fear of being overpowered. That is what belies their exterior personas.

I had fallen prey of what is called victimizing the victim based on the cohesion of a general consensus of persons who were too shallow, pig-headed, selfish, and scared to open their minds to effectively deal with my profound learning disability. I learned from my experiences that the cohesion of the "in" groups is more solidified when the outside party is blamed for any wrongdoings that may occur. This is called scapegoating.

One theory implies that people use scapegoating when a group is dis-gruntled by difficult issues, and they do not know how to handle mat-ters because of a lack of resources, or they are confronted with problems that they don't know how to resolve. When people are unable to rectify a problematic situation, they use a vulnerable target to take out their an-noyances on (Martin and Osborne 346-47).

I was a scapegoat because I was blamed for a profound condition that I was born with. I was taught to feel shame and guilt because I could not efficiently produce according to the standards that were imposed on me.

I was a fish out of water. I was deprived of the resources that I needed to flourish, and I was in an inappropriate environment.

However, someone had to take the blame. I was the sole member of a minority who didn't fit into the high profile status that people thought that I should have been in. I was clearly distinguishable from a powerful majority: poor grades; not excelling in sports; having few friends; having a hard time meeting girls; isolation standards; being mocked and teased, and simply following the beat of a different drummer. All of those factors made me safe to attack.

Continually pinning the blame on scapegoats may temporarily mitigate the woes and grievances of the victimizer, but the scapegoat remains the victim due to the ignorance of persons who fail to help the one who is being wrongly victimized (Martin and Osborne 347). I was cheated and victimized by ignorance the way others have been so by bigotry, racism, and anything else that fosters prejudice.

The ones who feel inferior may internalize the superior persons' perceptions and be vulnerable to creating self-fulfilling prophecies. These are derived from notions that they are inferior to begin with. Therefore, they will stay feeling inferior through what they think and do (347).

The self-fulfilling prophecy with my schoolwork came into being in the 6th and 7th grade in the prep school that I attended, and it grew worse and worse in the following years. I was among three other students who were contrasted with eight other students who did consistently well in one class. My teacher would say, "If I was to test you all, I could count on four of you to fail and the rest of you to pass and do very well." This negative reinforcement impinged my propensity to do well and work hard. However, there were times when I had done well on short-term levels; I had only done this to avoid any painful scolding, derision, and humiliation.

No matter what, I was wrongly victimized by the ignorance of many others, which generates prejudice.

Strange as it seems, prejudice has not always been so pervasive in every facet of life, even in the early 1800's. The Seminole Indians, who populated southern Georgia and all over the state of Florida, were very liberal, and they were the only people all over the world who accepted African Americans as the same as others. Seminoles reportedly offered sanctuaries to runaway slaves within their domain. African Americans were given their side of the land by the Seminoles within the designated area. They were slaves, but they were cared for and treated with dignity and respect as opposed to how the white man took care of them.

The Seminoles accepted interracial marriage relations with African Americans. Once these pacts were made an African American was welcome as a tribe member absolutely and without discussion (Stargell and Bird 1-2).

The point is, the potential to have open minds has probably existed longer than we can imagine; therefore, there has never been any excuse for prejudice/ignorance over education.

The story of the Seminoles and the African Americans exemplifies my theory. Obviously persons from long ago made it a policy to open their minds. More so, they were willing to cultivate and integrate persons from all walks of life and I presume that they were willing to learn from others and vice versa.

However, history has taught us that infinite dimensions of prejudice and hate have prevailed throughout the world and people are slighted, denied, and abused in the process. Progress has been made, but history has taught us that prejudice has not been obliterated (Martin and Osborne 344).

Though complete awareness of some issues may take a long time to develop, being obdurate about not keeping an open mind is still inexcusable. The same applies for the strife that I endured based on the ignorance of others.

I am not a parent, a certified teacher or a licensed social worker, even though I came close to earning a Master's degree in Agency Counseling. Not being a teacher or a research social scientist may not make me the most applicable person to make the most valid assessments. However, I have learned many things through my personal experiences, observations of others, and anything else that has enabled me to at least adequately teach the significance of keeping an open mind to all facets of life, since you can never do so perfectly.

Bias and prejudice are in all of us. None of us can deny that. No one will ever be completely free of it. There are no definite, inflexible methodologies to reduce prejudice on all levels. No one is perfect and everyone is human.

Sting once sang about how we are all human regardless of our personal thoughts and ideas. That is very true. Making a policy to keep an open mind may be the most essential component of becoming well educated. This ideology could help people come together and work with each other.

Theories have proven that when different groups collaborate with their personalities, talents and point of views, they provide new ways of doing things, and the integration of cultural experiences can become very beneficial for everyone (Axelson 14). It has been asserted, "the goal of a culturally pluralistic society is unity in diversity" (14).

The ingenuity of all individuals from all groups is crucial to the creation of vital resources to benefit everyone. Perceiving each individual as unique can more effectively eradicate the sinister spread of prejudice to establish a satisfactory level of intercultural fusion or pluralism.

Ethnic jokes or any jokes that connote stereotypes and anything grossly insensitive, should be emphasized as unacceptable and totally wrong on all levels.

I recall back in grade school when my teacher gave an assignment for students to tell Polish jokes. I was surprised by it then, and in retrospect, I am dismayed by it now. Jokes like that can be very damaging to anyone. Kids are certainly more encouraged to make politically incorrect jokes, especially if they hear them from their parents, teachers, or any other adults. I even heard jokes about the tragedy of the <u>Challenger</u> (the Space Shuttle explosion in 1986 with the seven astronauts) by formally educated adults when it happened.

Ethnic jokes especially encourage the group that tells them to be more unified. This isolates the group that is being belittled. This can, and does, reduce the dignities of the victimized groups, and it makes the group who is telling the joke more powerful on a collective plane (Martin and Osborne 350).

Parents and adults may knowingly or unwittingly encourage prejudicial thoughts and statements like a child saying "That man looks weird," because of the way he dresses or because he is overweight, then the parent or adult laughs and says "He sure does." It may seem harmless on the surface, but it can foster a more prejudiced attitude that would encourage the child to stereotype people rather than teaching the child to be more sensitive and more open minded (344).

Another example would be seeing a motorist in a car with a California license plate, then, one says "Where is his surfboard?" That may seem innocuous; however, it has the potential to encourage stereotyping, labeling, and prejudice. It can be very damaging and unjust to whoever is victimized by it.

We must concede that a child's surrounding environment and all of the persons within it influence his/her thoughts and feelings, which render any of their opinions and judgments.

Family factors are influential. These represent the initial group that each child generally comes in contact with. Children often model and even strive to emulate their parents and other significant adults who are charismatic to them when they are very young. If a father is disgruntled about how his tax dollars are being used to benefit welfare and food stamp recipients, and he becomes obsessively disenchanted with it, he could evoke a prejudiced attitude against them. If he expresses this attitude in front of his children, chances are, his children may emulate his actions and thoughts, even if they don't verbally express them. Children have tendencies to act in certain ways that are consistent with their parents (Martin and Osborne 344).

"Schools presumably teach children to play together and to get along well in groups" (344). However, quite often, there is little conscious consideration as to how institutions can formulate prejudiced attitudes in children. Teachers may inadvertently teach children to only play with certain children who may be categorized or labeled into distinguished groups (344-45).

Peer pressure is a colorful dimension that can be a breeding ground for prejudiced thoughts and behaviors, out of fear of being cast out or even worse, being taunted. Children's opinions about other children are influenced and shaped by their friends and/or peers. Groups come together and some are accepted and others are not. Children strive to emulate other children who appear to be the most powerful and charismatic (345). Experimental groups of students have been trained to think more critically to perceive persons as individuals and not judge them unfairly (348).

I recall a scenario from my freshman year at Bethany College in my Sociology of Social Problems class. The professor told all blue-eyed students to get on one side of the room, while the brown-eyed students got on the other side. At any rate, she praised the brown-eyed students, and she told them that they were bright and intelligent. She also told them that they would receive good grades in her class. Then the blue-eyed students were denounced by being told how sick we made her feel and that we were pathetic and stupid. We knew there was a point to this, even though we may have struggled to figure it out in the beginning. It was an exercise in teaching us the perils of discrimination. I think she reversed the situation in order for us to better understand the demonstration. Being college students, we were old enough to understand the exercise and we did not succumb to teasing each member of each group.

Numerous experiments have been conducted with children in elementary schools where teasing and taunting ensued, but teachers have stated that they were experiments to teach them how wrong it is to stereotype others, because it fosters prejudice, bias, and discrimination. Teachers and students reportedly find it to be worthy and beneficial to be involved with discrimination exercises (Martin and Osborne 345). Experiments such as these should be practiced on a more regular basis to instill the ideals of cooperation more than competition.

When children are more inclined to work together as a group to achieve a goal, chances are, each person will perceive the other person as a distinct individual. Then prejudice will more likely diminish (349).

I would guess that the age of 5 or 6 might be the earliest time to begin teaching children about wrongly judging others. There is nothing definite about that of course. Again, it may depend on the individual.

At any rate, we must foster the minds of our children with critically inquisitive minds, so they will be doubtful of ignorant statements, which formulate stereotypes. Children must be taught to see things as questionable. They must be trained to interpret the literal content of what is said and the way it is said (Martin and Osborne 348).

There is no absolute universal blueprint to prejudice proofing our children. So trying to force feed educational ideologies into children without giving them some independence to think for themselves is not a valid approach to teach what is bad about prejudice and ignorance.

If kids feel that they are being pushed around into thinking what is politically correct without being taught to think for themselves, they may become resentful and have no inclination to reduce prejudiced thoughts and to stop making prejudiced statements. Children must experience things for themselves in order to think for themselves.

If a child makes a racial slur or any ignorant comment, and a parent or teacher reprimands them by saying "I'm really disappointed in you" or "You should know better than that," rather than "You are so despicable" they will better understand how wrong what they said was, learn from it, and be more careful not to let it happen again. If the latter approach is used, it benefits no one. If our children are taught these skills in a way, which enhances them to practice them on a regular basis, they will less likely behave with prejudiced thoughts.

We must take into account that prejudicial comments are made to get attention. Even if you relentlessly bicker with a prejudiced person to make that person understand his/her ignorance, it is a way of attention seeking on the prejudiced person's part, who may feel ironically gratified; hence, maintain his/her prejudiced thoughts (Martin and Osborne 350).

It seems that the best way to reduce prejudice is to turn the cold shoulder from it consistently (even though you can't do so completely). You can do this by turning away and leaving, talking about something different, or simply refusing to concede what they say by giving no verbal nor non-verbal responses (350).

We must acknowledge that prejudice does exist. Nevertheless, you must move beyond guilt and be committed to make a greater future instead of musing through your personal contrition of the past. Empowering yourself through education can enable you to inspire individuals to positively make changes for themselves.

We must be proactive not just politically, but we must get involved with any educational modalities to correct unfair situations and problems, rather than being reactive. In other words, we must walk the walk as well as talk the talk to correct anything that is wrong. If we don't, we are just as irresponsible as the persons who are guilty of any wrongdoings if we simply moan and groan about what grieves us. We simply must take affirmative action to rectify anything through education.

CHAPTER FIVE

Education

"If you think education is costly, try ignorance"

— *Unknown*

Education is defined as "development in knowledge, skill, ability, or character by teaching, training, study, or experience; teaching; training" (Thorndike and Barnhart 321).

Education is a term with relative meanings, and it should not always connote specific uniform institutions of thought, but sadly, it often does.

The more that you are willing to open your mind to anything and everything in life, the more educated you become regardless of how you had done in your formative years in school, where you went to college, what you majored in, what your GPA was, your SAT, ACT, GRE scores, and so forth. Education is relative regardless of how it is defined in the dictionary.

Someone said that "Education is not preparation for life, education is life." I could not agree with that more. I believe that when one acknowledges his/her personal uniqueness, it helps inspire one to learn and grow to become a well-rounded individual. Theodore Roosevelt proclaimed **"That what matters is what you do with what you have where you are."**

Intelligence is varied and subjective. Howard Gardner argued that there are 8 different dimensions (Mooney and Cole 69). The late J.P. Guilford asserted that there were 120 distinct intellectual dimensions (Lyman 39).

I.Q. tests and other criteria are used to supposedly measure one's present intelligence to predict future performance levels. They are just tools to come up with the best possible conclusions that they can. They are administered by supposedly well-educated professionals, who are just as human as everyone else (not the least bit perfect). They can only infer so much and there are often errors (Lyman 9-10).

Informal educational standards that are imparted to you can be personally enriching to the individual more than you can imagine. It can stem from heart-to-heart one-on-one-discussions with family members; teacher to student; supervisor to supervisee; colleague to colleague; friend to friend; acquaintance to acquaintance, and so forth.

There is no essential, one-dimensional learning style for all individuals. Unfortunately, the opposite notion has been purported in too many circles. That is a dreadful factor of ignorance in our educational and professional settings (Mooney and Cole 69).

Thinking and preaching that everyone learns the same way and treating others as such, is a generalized sample of ignorance. Remaining in restrictive environments without reaching out to others to interact with other forms of life can foster more ignorance than education. It could enhance one to make shallow judgements, because they are not engaging with life to see what else might actually be out there.

Kids do not develop in the same linear, sequential manner. No one size fits all. Some are late bloomers (Mooney and Cole 69). I used to be one of them. Nevertheless, I didn't question it; I blindly rolled with it. I was taught that Math, Science, and all of the traditional fundamentals (culturally based) were more important than creative art/practical ideas.

Many critical minded educators think that kids absorb and comprehend ideas in a number of ways such as auditory, oral, "tactile, kinesthetic, verbal, visual, spatial, and project based" modalities (69).

Creativity is an essential element of education. However, it is discredited for the most part, because we are led to believe that the mainstream fundamentals in our oppressive school systems are what count, even if students betray and repress their gifts, which are all part of their unique individualities. Creative thought can be so much more beneficial to the individual and who he/she comes in contact with (75).

An example would be a dyslexic student named David Cole, co-author of <u>Learning Outside The Lines</u>. Cole had an unorthodox interview in the admissions office at Brown University. He used an arrangement of steel sculptures that were held together on a coffee table. It was his writing course of action and he explained it. He was accepted (60).

I think everyone is wise enough to know that people have strengths and talents regardless of how unique and deviant they may appear to others as a whole. However, declaiming those attributes and standards as though they do not count, because they are not part of the traditional curriculums in most schools, is a major injustice to any individual. If you say that those qualities do not count and that they are unimportant, what you are basically telling the individuals is that they are not important! How could that be?

If you value and cherish people and children who live in the world, and you want them to be well-rounded, then you have to acknowledge that these persons are unique and special to begin with. You should be able to understand that because you too are unique and special. Children are that way from the moment that they are born!

When you realize the mere existence of human beings, then you know that they certainly matter, because they need to live, survive, and be given the opportunities to be in appropriate environments, so they can do the best that they can with what they have. That, of course, does not mean give them anything and everything that they want without instructing them to earn it.

However, it is so terribly hypocritical to criticize and punish persons especially those, who are as challenged as I, when they are unable to produce because they are not provided with the tools and resources to be efficient. That is scapegoating, which can lead to persons blindly following authoritative figures, the same way sheep follow a shepherd. Children should not be abused or cursed if they do not belong in a setting that is inappropriate to their educational and emotional needs.

Creative and practical thinkers deserve to be in appropriate environments, and some persons may need to be educated in places that enable them to learn how to learn. For some people, that can take a long time. It certainly did for me because I was denied the privileges and resources that I needed. Some people are late bloomers to begin with, and they should not feel ashamed of that, especially when they eventually learn and comprehend things.

Fortunately, these days, people are becoming more aware of individuals with conditions such as mine, and there seems to be more effort being made to accommodate them. Still, many people are denied opportunities to use and demonstrate their unique talents when people are unwilling to provide resources for them, and they are not perceived as unique individuals to begin with. Some are denied the love they need as individuals as well as the opportunities to transcend with their personal gifts, just because they may represent so-called minority groups.

If everyone is unique, and the things that they engage in are unique, then educational systems in themselves should be expansive and welcoming of diversity, rather than adhering to limited traditional norms that unfairly determine the overall quality of a solid education.

If individuals lack other essentials that make an education so valuable, then the purpose of what an overall education is really supposed to be about is defeated. When the tools and resources are not provided to help one succeed, the individual can miss out on understanding what education is about when he/she cannot adequately engage with it. When I attended my prep school, syllabuses were never provided when they should have been. They are golden resources for one to efficiently prepare and do well. I know this from my college and graduate school experiences.

Of course, even if my former prep school had provided syllabuses, I still would have done poorly on the whole, because I was somewhere that I didn't belong: **A FISH OUT OF WATER!!!!!** Nevertheless, these thorough guidelines that specifically instruct you on what and how to prepare, can help others succeed. It did so for me when I was at Bethany and when I attended Graduate School.

If each school project is different with different information and every one learns differently, then reviews and preparations should be made. Accommodations were rarely provided for me. Accommodations must be made for every distinct individual who needs them. I had these accommodations when I was at Bethany. However, I did not abuse these privileges and I only used them if and when I thought that they were absolutely necessary, which was seldom. I made it a policy to be fair, not just to prevent others from holding grudges against me, but also because I knew in my heart, that I should do what was right.

Grades are really just letters and numbers that indicate how you have performed in certain areas. Many persons who have done well in school have been unsuccessful in life. This can come from a lack of ambition, being pampered or spoiled, being shallow and prejudiced, or being guilty of any rebellious and destructive behavior.

Time constraints, multitudes of priorities, family distractions, opposite sex relations, environmental factors, and just the different, specific ways that people learn things, should always be taken into consideration when assessing one's learning potential.

Academic outcasts are often denounced and put out to pasture as losers, weirdoes, and freaks. The school I attended could not possibly be at fault, right? Wrong! Of course, the school was not entirely at fault. No one listens to these people until it is too late; For example, The Columbine High School Massacre (Mooney and Cole 65-66).

Despite positive changes that are being made and ones that are threatening to be made, society and perhaps even the media seem to emphasize the traditional fundamentals that have constituted our school systems through the years such as science, math, social studies, English, history, and foreign languages. In some school circles, there does not seem to be as much of an expansive regard for radio and television classes, theater and acting, drama classes, home economics/culinary arts, and exclusive creative writing classes, all of which should be treated with equal emphasis.

It would be nice if there were more expansive art classes, such as sculpture and ceramics or more exclusive music classes, such as classical and jazz guitar and piano, or violin, and vocal classes. Exclusive carpentry classes for students may be good to incorporate into curriculums. Exclusive courses in geology, astronomy, or even astrology would widen the gamut for a solid education in any academic setting.

Extracurricular activities such as clubs can also incline students to get involved; if there are enough that are suitable to the uniqueness of every individual. Athletics is another area, which should be broadened enough for students who may have a multitude of interests. Unfortunately, many people favor the more traditionally appreciated sports, such as football and basketball, as opposed to soccer or lacrosse, though soccer is catching up in popularity. Still, many people take these sports for granted, because they favor the more traditional ones.

I know that it is difficult to govern a school system that is always filled with bureaucratic red tape. However, if education is to benefit everyone, then everyone should be judged as unique individuals with unique gifts and needs. That is how education begins, by simply opening the mind to anything and everything. If you write off anything as insignificant without even giving it any thought from the start, you defeat the whole purpose of what education is all about.

I know that it may be difficult to incorporate some diverse dimensions into our schools. This may come from an overall lack of interest from individuals in communities as a whole. I am also aware that garnering enough funds to finance some of these things can be very difficult, because of restrictive state and federal government budgets. Persons voting against taxes to finance more of these diverse areas to accommodate a seemingly precious few individuals can be a problem. Nevertheless, if education is life, which it most certainly is, everyone should listen to any ideas and keep them in mind.

I know that people claim that they appreciate diversity in people and things in life, and some people may truly believe that they do, but sadly, many do not.

Some persons who may grow up in areas that profoundly lack an appreciation of diversity and variety, such as the one I grew up in, can encourage others to maintain their norms, which may seem so predictably linear, constrictive, and shallow in scope.

I want to make it clear that there are many good things about the area where I grew up. I am living not too far outside of it now. It is a great place to raise a family if you can afford to do so. It is an hour from Pittsburgh, a major city that I love. There is diversity in the area, but you may have to ambitiously develop a more perceptive eye to discover some of it. Nonetheless, it has a relatively homogenized mainstream of persons who have very similar interests such as high school sports, and a limited regard for theater and arts. There is nothing wrong with the community's love of sports, but there is more to life than that. Just because the area has been that way traditionally, does not invariably excuse having a limited gamut of intercultural events.

What is so notoriously prevalent in our society is how our educational system distinguishes between who is in and who is out; the haves and the have nots; the smart and stupid, and the athletic and unathletic. Much of it is based on grades and sport letters, which presumably indicate and determine the worthiness of each individual.

One of the worst myths of all is that if you constantly work hard a majority of the time, whether your grades are good or not, you will be invariably well-educated, especially if you attend any elite private schools. That theory couldn't be more asinine.

Some things appear deceptively good on a superficial level such as GPA's, test scores (standardized tests), achievements, and awards in extracurricular activities. Assessing students as being lazy and inferior is superficial and wrong (Lyman 41). I learned this the hard way when I went through torturous hell at my prep school for seven years.

My Old Prep School - Glory Days - NOT!!!!!

One shallow teacher that I had at this prep school said that it was a shame that students had trouble learning.

One particular teacher made a sport of roaring at students and verbally abusing them. The real shame was and is that there is so much ignorance that champions the oppressive school structures. More so, teachers and administrators claim that their methods are the right ways; therefore, the students' rate of success is contingent on how significant authority figures in the school judge them.

One thing that dismayed me terribly was how many teachers at the prep school that I attended, would maliciously criticize the local public and catholic schools by telling us that if you want to laugh and not have to study, go to those other schools. The teachers stressed the names of those schools adamantly. We were told that we would not learn anything at those schools compared to what you learn at the prep school even though those schools had broader curriculums comprised of more diverse classes. Other statements were "You'll have a tough time in college if you transfer to the public school" and "You'll regret it." That makes sense, right? **It most certainly does not!!**

Some teachers at this school would humiliate students who would wrongly answer questions and criticize them if they tried to clarify things that they were not sure of. Some were mocked and taunted at random about things that bore no relevance to the class, such as the color of a shirt that a student was wearing, the ways some students walked, being overweight, having large noses and cheeks, and many other things. Those factors encouraged the pupils to regularly snicker and pick on the students.

Some students were compared and contrasted with each other to signify who was superior or inferior. One teacher scoffingly revealed to another student how a student with a learning disability misspelled a word. There's nothing amusing about someone who may have a spelling disability, and that teacher had no business disclosing that information to another student. It was simply none of his business.

One teacher wrote a list of announcements for a student to read over an intercom for the student body and teachers to hear. The German club was supposed to meet at a certain time during the day, but the message read that the "Craut" club was to meet. The student read it based on what the teacher had written. What a fine example that set for a large group of students embodying a learning establishment!

Ignorance just continues and continues to prevail.

Ignorance is the opposite of education and some teachers I had known encouraged the kids to be shallow and viciously insulting. Is that what education is all about? Education should not encourage persons to be arrogant, two-faced, hypocritical, and verbally and physically abusive.

Believe me, there were teachers who made fun of students and consciously encouraged other students to do so in the process. There were teachers who had their favorite pets and they let them goof off. These teachers were inordinately generous to those selected individuals at the expense of others.

The school's general philosophy was that they did not want to hear any excuses about students who were having a hard time. They just told us to keep studying harder and harder and that was it. It did not matter how much they bombarded us with massive quantities of assignments without any adequate preparation for them.

The school claimed to the public that individuality was equally emphasized whether or not a student was a jock or a member of the band. The real agenda of the school was to bureaucratically govern a collective powerhouse of a school that exploited the students through political machinations based on a financial principle. In other words, it was an ugly lie, which is an essential element of anything that has a ruthless political infrastructure.

After all, it is a private school, and if students do something that is bad within the confines of the school, but it is not so severe that it could warrant an expulsion, it is kept within the "family boundaries." However, if a student does something naughty outside the school, the student is reprimanded for political reasons, because they fear that it could make the school look bad as a whole. This was done rather than disciplining the student in a logical and practical way to educate him about how wrong he was.

More so, the individuals were rarely shown how much they were cared for about their growth as individuals and what they could do to improve upon some things.

Furthermore, it is even more wrong for teachers to pick on students when they know they are struggling, but they randomly and ruthlessly call on them anyway, especially if an individual student's weaknesses are exposed to the rest of the classmates. When I was in college and graduate school, I was seldom called on with the exception of a few occasions when I was expected to know something, but I was not cursed for it if I did not know the answer.

Teachers claim that they are just trying to be fair when they do that by treating everyone the same. That is fine if you are equally courteous, respectful, cordial, and commending of everyone with whom you come in to contact, and you acknowledge them as unique individuals who may have unique strengths, weaknesses, and different learning styles.

When I attended the prep school, deficiency reports were ruthlessly distributed to the parents, faculty, advisors, and even the teachers who did not teach specific students who were deficient. Kids like me were stigmatized by these reports. Some students may have improved on a short-term level, just to alleviate any current humiliation, but in the long run, they remained bitter, angry, resentful, and defiant of learning when they struggled. I know that some were angry because they were denied the opportunities to develop and utilize their unique talents, because they were not emphasized enough in the curriculum. Therefore, it was not a broad based education. Students were forced to conform to what was supposedly more important, and if they alienated and repressed talents which were perceived as anomalies, too bad. They would simply have to take their lumps as I had.

One factor that I learned was that when people do come a long way and do very well, they are still belittled by their detractors and enemies by certain statements. The following are some:

- *"It's about time"*

- *"I'm sure glad it did not take you long to do it right this time like it had before"*

- *"I wish he knew his Civics as well as he knew his sports trivia"*

- *"Hooray, he finally made it"*

Those were demeaning statements that were made to me by my teachers and peers. I observed those kinds of things in others who were put down similarly. Of course, their confidence levels diminished as mine had, especially when I, and others realized that we had to spend so much time on one thing, and not enough on others, and we became unprepared to answer questions in class.

I remember one of my English teachers in high school stating that if students were not prepared for class each day to answer questions from reading assignments, then, they should not even bother coming to class. **What kind of garbage is that?!?**

When I was in graduate school, I had gotten behind on the reading assignments for a class that we were not tested on until much later, because I spent more time on more pressing matters that demanded more immediate deadlines such as tests, research papers, and the like. Of course, my profound learning disability had a great deal to do with it. However, I went to every class and I earnestly took copious notes to catch up, even though I was not sufficiently prepared to answer questions. Once I had more time, I went back to everything and I put all of it together. I aced the final and I earned an A in the class. I even earned my first 4.0 ever. So who can accuse me of being lazy and apathetic; just like many others who were wrongly accused as such in this particular English class.

The main point is, this former English teacher of mine was viewing his students on a collective level rather than an individualized one. He failed to acknowledge that everyone is unique, and he did not concede that some students, myself included, may not have belonged in this particular setting. Of course, he did not sufficiently prepare us for tests, just like many other teachers irresponsibly did not.

Therefore, no one should feel shame for not being able to catch up and stay on top of everything, let alone, do well in school. Poor teaching skills may actually be the real problem, especially if a majority of a class fails the same test, including the honor students.

I want to make it clear that there were some good teachers at this school who perceived students as unique individuals and they were compassionate and respectful of them. My biology teacher might have been the best one. I am sorry that they have to read this, but they should know very well that there is no excuse for any disgraceful accusations, humiliation, and abuse in an educational environment.

Pink Floyd:
"Another Brick In The Wall (Part 2)"

This is an analogy from Pink Floyd's rock opera <u>The Wall</u>. Contrary to popular belief, the song does not rebel against education. It is totally the opposite (Jones 125). The song is derived from Roger Waters, the primary composer of the band and opera, who had bad experiences in an elite school filled with some cruel teachers that administered austere methods to make the students sufficiently produce in a seemingly standardized way. Waters, who tended to dispute the teachers styles' was terribly mortified by one when he attended this school. This scenario is conveyed in a semi-autobiographical sequence in the film of <u>The Wall</u> (124-25).

I was a victim of these kinds of experiences and I understand Waters's perspective on it. Therefore, I share his sentiments most dogmatically. Also, like Waters, he claimed that there were some teachers at his school that were very kind and decent, as there were at the prep school that I attended (124-25).

I was confronted with what is called "factory schooling." This is denoted in a surrealistic way in the film to manifest how the students go one by one into a huge grinder in a linear, mainstreamed fashion. They become transmogrified to signify how hollow and spiritually impoverished they become. They appear faceless, miserable, and filled with nothingness. They are connoted as having no unique individualities and no personal enrichment. They don't feel inspired by education whether they perform efficiently or not (Giannetti 198).

Some of those factors stem from the students not feeling encouraged to think critically for themselves. As a result, the students become reluctant of education and they revolt against it. Furthermore, when teachers abuse students through more negative reinforcement and destructive criticism rather than using positive reinforcement and constructive criticism, they do not heighten one's propensity to learn. Instead, a student suppresses it (Jones 125).

You see, jumping through someone else's political hoops without thinking critically for yourself and charting your own path contradicts what education is about.

Learning Outside of the Classroom

I firmly believe that you learn more outside of the classroom than you do inside, because life and the world in which we live are comprised of so much richness and diversity. If you are deprived or simply don't take advantage of opportunities to learn about life, you cheat yourself from becoming the most well-rounded individual that you can be. Of course, if you make it a policy to read often, and to occasionally watch educational television programs on <u>Discovery</u>, the <u>History Channel</u>, <u>CNN</u>, etc. these educational mediums can enlighten you as well. Nevertheless, social interactions with people in any situation, whether it be attendance at educational functions such as visiting museums and art galleries, or taking field trips, certainly enable one to learn and grow. Any experiences that you have enhance you to learn and grow.

Experiential Learning

Perhaps, one of the primary ways of becoming well-educated and educating others is to reach out and communicate with fellow human beings through extensive, personal interactive experiences, no matter what the cost. Experiential learning can be better assimilated than classroom lectures.

A good example of this comes from a famous former policeman named David Toma. Two television programs were based on his life <u>Toma</u> and <u>Baretta</u> (Toma and Levey 5). Before he became a law enforcement officer, he had the same prejudiced, narrow view of street junkies as many others had. He was appalled by them, and he thought that they were an insult to decent society (11).

Despite, Mr. Toma's dismay, he was determined to learn everything that he could about these people. Once he did, he perceived them much differently. He said that he sometimes saw emptiness in these people, which may have signified that they wanted to be treated and healed. The feelings that caused Mr. Toma to reach out and help them had grown so immensely, he was in too deep to turn back (12).

The pain of the junkies connoted a yearning to be loved, and the more Mr. Toma moved forward and took chances to reach out to them, the more educated he became. That is what life is about. The more Mr. Toma reached out to interact and communicate with others, the more he enhanced his learning potential. More than that, he was more willing to become acquainted with the remote, minute, underlying factors that may have contributed to these kids' indulging in drugs and their inevitable deteriorations (12).

Toma said that many of these kids were not from the projects and slums. Not all of these kids had parents who were drug addicts, alcoholics, prostitutes, and the like. Many of them came from very prosperous socioeconomic backgrounds. Many of these kids were probably very happy and took life as it happened when they were little (16).

Toma implied that society does not have a drug problem because of the easy accessibility of drugs. He said that people become hooked because they can't effectively deal with their lives. They are looking to run away, so they turn to alcohol and drugs to ease the pain. These individuals can't handle issues with loved ones, employers, peers, teachers, their lives of love, or culture. They have low self-esteem and feel like nobody loves them or wants them. They can't bear the thought of the future. He said that these people are lonely and despondent, and they are convinced that nobody cares to lend them a helping hand (27).

Basically, I think Mr. Toma's rhetoric was that these people, along with others, lacked the sufficient resources to cope with the dreadfully cold starkness of reality. Therefore, if people were willing to open their eyes and minds more, they would not only better understand what the problems are, but they may also feel more obligated to help people the best way that they can based on what they learn through any form of experiential education.

Toma's theory is underscored more with Roger Waters of Pink Floyd. Waters was raised by his mother, who was reportedly an ardent social activist, helping many disadvantaged persons who lived in her community. She reportedly inspired her son with some strong humanistic principles. In regard to the homeless people suffering out in the cold, in Cliff Jones's book, <u>Another Brick in the Wall</u>, Waters proclaims by rhetorically asking "are they on the streets because they're worthless, shifty, no good, useless, anti-social ingrates? No, they're on the street because they can't cope. They are displaced and they need looking after" (100).

The Potential to Learn is Infinite

You hear people say, "I have been doing this for many years; therefore, there is nothing that I don't know, so I don't need someone half my age trying to lecture me." Persons may boast about their formal educational backgrounds, and the number of degrees they have earned, to justify their unwillingness to listen to any innovative ideas. However, there are many who do acknowledge that they have the potential to learn even more; therefore, they would be open to new ideas or anything that they are not necessarily well educated about.

Paradigm Shifts

Paradigm shifts happen in the business world because people know that if they are going to efficiently compete in a dog-eat-dog world, they must be willing to evolve otherwise they inevitably devolve and stagnate. We all learned how the Swiss watch industry was unwilling to modify some things to stay in business, so they went belly up because the American/Japanese watch industry heeded the calls of the public, and thrived.

As we know, the world is made up of unique individuals, with the economic world composed of commodities. Of course, we know that these goods are to be bought and sold. The consumers who buy them are unique individuals and they often know what they want. The expression "The customer is always right" comes from that theory, because if the business is not willing, nor able to provide what the customer wants, they won't make money. That's a no-brainer.

If people want to make money, which many do, they need to be aware of what others like, and if they acknowledge that everyone is unique, they will be more inclined to come up with ideas for producing goods that satisfy the individual customers' needs. I know that is easier said than done. Nevertheless, it is a factor that cannot be ignored.

I think one of the most significant factors of education besides keeping an open mind, is being flexible, not necessarily to completely change who and what you are, but to learn about new things and try them out. This can make people more stimulated by other new ideas and more fascinated with what is going on in the world rather than being bored all of the time (O'Connor and Seymour 5).

Many persons are unwilling to change because they are so hung up with maintaining the status quo, which is often due to uncompromisingly conventional standards that people have been accustomed to for many years. Sure, it can be hard to adjust to some new changes especially if they are spontaneous. However, many people are too immersed in their traditional norms to make any paradigm shifts. Some people fear change on a dramatic level, not just because they may fear being ostracized, but because when they are set in their own ways, they do not want to change them (Dyer 117-18, 124).

Since education is a life-long process that enriches one's mind, there is no excuse for one to say at any particular point "I don't need to pay attention to all of that or make any changes." Being open to innovative ideas for business as well as educational and spiritual purposes, not only helps one to be more appreciative of what he/she learns, but, it inclines one to be more willing and interested in what life has to offer.

Education Through Painful Awareness

Of course, part of being well-educated is being more aware of the perilous rigors of life, which are ever so harsh and grim. Some persons who attended a traditional four-year liberal arts college may arguably be more prepared to deal with reality (and that's debatable), but they will realize how hard it is once they get into the real world. I have learned that no one is 100% prepared for the real world after graduating from college. However, in some circles, there may be more of a dependency on college educated and graduate school students to provide what is needed for others, so they can live prosperously in a viable society. People often depend on the college educated people to produce and sustain a well-governed democratic society.

During my Bethany College commencement, Edward Albee, an international renowned playwright, was the guest speaker. He told us that we had been "deeply wounded by education, and he said that we must keep our wounds open and not let scar tissue develop over them." I think his point was that despite the personal enrichments that we may have acquired from the college experience, part of being educated involves the grim exposure and interaction with the hardships of reality, which all of us inevitably face. This goes to show that we keep on learning and learning.

Don't Beat Yourself Up
When You Don't Know Something

I believe that many people feel guilty and humiliated whenever they realize that they did not know something that they think they should have known. Most can relate to this, but persons holding bachelors', masters', law, Ph.Ds, and medical degrees also can also relate to this. It is quite amazing what some people know and others do not based on their educations, backgrounds, culture and any variable elements that would be considered relative.

I have felt guilty many times myself for things that I think that I should have known, but I remind myself that everyone has the infinite potential to learn and nobody knows everything. Since we are all born with weaknesses and strengths, we should accept that we will never know everything. We should all accept that some intellectual voids will never be filled.

People with college degrees may miss some very colorful things they should have learned whether they be the Boston Massacre or the burning of witches in Salem, Massachusetts.

Regardless of whether we have extreme difficulty absorbing and retaining information, we must remain inclined to learn more, but at the same time, accept ourselves and others as being merely human. We are not perfect, and our capacities to be well educated, though expansive in nature, are ironically limited because we are merely human. Our humanities also allow us to live a life that does not invariably require academics and professional work alone.

Basically we all need to have **fun**, interact with others, share the love, and be creative in other aspects outside of school and work. According to Jonathan Mooney and David Cole, authors of <u>Learning Outside the Lines</u>, "School develops and values less than 10% of what it means to be human and to live a full life" (247).

One of the most significant theories that I wish to preach is that all of us are human beings, so we must acknowledge that we all need to relax, enjoy ourselves, and have a good time. This may be the most crucial thing we can teach our children. We adults must remind ourselves of this.

Sure, academics and work come first before rest and play, but if you truly want your kids to feel happy, adequate, useful, and loved, you must emphasize to them that grades, honors, promotions, bonuses, and possessions etc. are secondary factors, which are an insignificant part of each unique individual.

Telling your kids that they must succeed in everything that they do, no matter what the cost, is a brutal misconception that can psychologically damage a child for life.

One of my best friends was having a terribly difficult time at the prep school that I attended, and he was doing absolutely nothing but studying and running cross-country, yet he continued to do very poorly. He told some key authoritative figures at the school that there was more to life than just studying all of the time. He was having no life or barely any life, just like me, and I had at least ten times or even more major difficulty than he had.

My friend made a very important decision. He courageously transferred to a public school. It turned out to be one of the best moves he ever made. From that point on, his life started to change for the better and forever. He made the honor roll and he was accepted into a good college, at which he had done very well. He is now married to a wonderful person and he is leading a Christian life that has brightened his life more than words can say. So much for grades, letters, numbers, test scores, trophies, and any other overt components that wrongly define everything about one's competence, efficiency, and, may I add: **CHARACTER!!!!**

We can do our best more when we are actually enjoying life whether it is at work, rest, or play.

Competition is a good thing as long as it does not override cooperation on all levels. One of the crucial elements of this theory is to admit that everyone is unique, regardless therefore, we must develop more perceptive eyes and ears to unique underlying factors that make all persons what they are. We must cooperate with others before we try to get kids and students to compete.

I encourage everyone involved to be open to these issues. Parents, taxpayers, teachers, principals/headmasters, superintendents, school board members, PTA's, politicians, lawyers, and anyone else should think about what I have imparted to you.

Think about grants to provide funds to finance counseling and special advising programs, and other diverse programs and activities that have the potential to accommodate everyone. Be careful not to make harsh accusations about one being lazy and negligent based on test results in school, or any setting without trying to be objective. A person may very well have problems similar to mine or worse.

Other integral components that are sometimes needed to succeed are loans to pay for college that not only enable one to attend college but more importantly, succeed in it.

Education can be used as a means to liberate yourself, especially if you identify yourself for who you truly are, whether or not you have an alternative learning style. It makes no difference, regardless (Mooney and Cole 23).

Most people need an education that provides an opportunity to excel, feel empowered, and be free. The more educated persons become to empower themselves at a young age the more they can evolve as individuals to use whatever skills they have. This can help significant others see what they can do rather than the opposite.

Failing is Educational

Failures and setbacks should paradoxically be emphasized as good learning points, because they can compel you to work harder for compensation. You are going to fail at times no matter what, not just because you might have had an extraordinarily profound condition such as mine, but even more so, if you were unfairly displaced like I was before my Bethany College years.

Job applications, cover letters, interviews, communications skills, extensive vocabulary, color and verbal processing, pragmatic learning, and project based learning should be underscored and embraced on all levels.

We will never actually succeed in life if we do not allow ourselves to fall down sometimes. That is what is called learning lessons.

Failure should be a right for all people. The more people see that everyone is unique and not everyone learns and performs at the same pace and rate, people will understand that they can still perform efficiently somehow. They will then have better chances of succeeding as a result.

Learning From Our Children

Communicating with children in nurturing, coddling fashions can induce kids to be more open about what they value. This makes them feel special and unique. Children can teach you more than you know. They not only unveil their talents, but they wish to talk about them gleefully. They may reveal interesting educational qualities and character traits about themselves that may appear to be unusual at times, but if we keep an open mind about them and think in terms of reciprocally learning from them rather than thinking that we need to only teach them, our children will grow and benefit. If you are unwilling to keep those principles in mind, you can adversely affect children psychologically.

The Need for Counseling

Counseling services should be in every school. We all know that kids are not always going to be happy especially if they are struggling in school. Telling them to "Get over it," "Quit crying," and "Stop feeling sorry for yourself" are demeaning statements that merely embitter a student to feel immobilized and isolated, which furthers more and more emotional distress. Many persons, myself included, were deprived of counseling resources. The necessity of these resources cannot be underscored enough.

Emotional support is at least equally vital for everyone. Treating people like robots doesn't exemplify what education is all about. Teaching that everyone needs love and to be themselves can be one of the most educational things you can do. Criticizing and vehemently lecturing kids about studying all of the time is a degrading misconception, mainly because it is a load of idiotic trash!!

Physically and verbally intimidating your kids and students to be more efficient could not be more wrong. There were many corrupt actions that I witnessed at my prep school: kids being slammed up against walls;

kicked in the shins; hit in the chest or back; and slapped in the backs of their heads. Other examples consisted of viciously chastising students verbally, with put downs, insults, names/labels, sarcastic, condescending remarks, and belittling innuendoes.

Just because students earn good grades, or excel in sports and extra-curricular activities, or frequently socialize with others, doesn't necessarily mean that a student cannot be depressed or is not in any need need of emotional comfort. Emotional comfort can be derived from compassion, understanding, and empathy.

When you open your eyes and mind to life through education, you open your heart more to anything in life. Therefore, you gain compassion, understanding, and empathy, which make up the next chapter.

To conclude this chapter, I encourage you to read and/or listen to the lyrics to the second verse of a song by The Who entitled "In a Hand or a Face." The song is from <u>The Who By Numbers</u> album and the lyrics are available on many websites of The Who on the internet, which contain discography tabs.

The author of the song, Pete Townshend guitarist and composer of The Who, had written the song at a time when he apparently had an imbalance of compassionate and empathic thoughts and feelings of people who struggled, and contemptuous thoughts and feelings of other people, whom he found to be cold, shallow, and aloof (Swenson 4).

Please read the second verse. It challenges you to become better educated with compassion, understanding, and empathy. It is even more compelling when you listen to the lyrics and music. If you do check this out, read it and listen to it carefully and don't take it for granted. Let it resonate through your mind.

CHAPTER SIX

Compassion, Understanding & Empathy

We all know that from the moment a child is born, it immediately needs tender loving care and compassion, because we understand that it is helpless, fragile, and vulnerable. We know that other species, including domestic and feral breeds of life, have emotions that enable them to love their offspring. This is because they understand that their young need compassion and love, as they need love in return. All mammals, whether they are human or not, are in need of that. More importantly, we all have understanding because we consciously or even subconsciously are empathic of others especially those who are in dire need of help and love. And as we know, babies constitute the essence of that.

I talked about cooperation in the previous chapter, which fosters the concepts of compassion, understanding, and empathy on a much more lucid level. Some of the most essential components of being well educated are having compassion, understanding, and empathy. I think the sooner you bestow this on your children in a way that they will understand it, the more inclined they may be to express it to others.

However, everyone is unique. There are no guidelines to instill children with compassion, understanding, and empathy toward every person and living organism on the face of the Earth. You simply need to use your own discretion as to when, what, and how you would do so. This would come through endless trial and error, which is what life is basically about.

Compassion is the sorrow for the sufferings of others. Having compassion helps you realize that you should not be ashamed of your weaknesses. You understand this more when you get involved in things, like cleaning up the environment, helping the poor and needy, and doing volunteer time in rest homes or any handicapped networks.

Understanding is the comprehension to reason and distinguish with knowledge and sympathy. Understanding relies upon the ability to observe and develop ideas in the mind. Empathy involves putting yourself completely in the position of another and expressing his/her feelings and actions in some creative manner.

Authored by Carl Rogers, <u>A Way of Being</u> gives very exquisite definitions of the word empathy: "means entering the private perceptual world of the other and becoming thoroughly at home in it. It involves being sensitive, moment by moment, to the changing felt meanings, which flow in this other person" (142). "In some sense it means that you lay aside yourself; this can only be done by persons who are secure enough in themselves that they know they will not get lost in what may turn out to be the strange or bizarre world of the other" (143). Rogers adds "empathy dissolves alienation" (151).

An empathic way of being can be learned from empathic persons. We must strive to understand one's point of view on things. Being empathic is a communication mode to one's thoughts and feelings. One can purport more appreciation and understanding by assisting others to think more deeply about things which bolsters you do to so as well. This gives you more of an incentive to remove barriers that hinder communication, and then, communicate more freely about anything that troubles you. As a result, you will be more willing to communicate about anything that interests you, so you can share knowledge, ideas, and anything else that helps you relate to others.

From the moment a child is born, you are compelled to nourish the child with so much compassion, understanding, and empathy to not only take care of the baby but love it. We know from that point on, that every child needs those attributes to survive, live well, and be happy. Of course, you can only coddle a child for so long, especially when the child grows up. Nevertheless, that does not mean that you just throw away the ideals of practicing these three attributes with your children and anyone else that you come in contact with. We all know that every human being has weaknesses. Since everyone is a unique individual, we should understand that everyone has strengths. People should have the compassion and wisdom to understand that.

Teachers and counselors that work with kids with ADHD say they have the ability to be very empathic with others, which stems from their sensitivities, which are distinct attributes that compel them to feel deep sympathy and understanding for others who are plagued by different things.

Conceding weaknesses at young ages can challenge children to transcend them. I have learned that if adults take the time to communicate with children to find out what they like to do and what makes them feel special, they can do wonders to raise that child's self-esteem. That of course, can help renew the firing power within children to enhance any creative passions that they may have for learning.

Regardless of our specific political views, we want to change our lives and the lives of others for the better. This enables us to have compassion and understanding. When people feel enriched by brightening the lives of others who struggle and need help, nothing can measure up to what you have done to empower those who you are helping.

It is important to make kids understand that when they are born with deficits, they can only be the best that they can be. They should not be cursed by people, who lack the patience and education to accept them for who and what they are.

One should not be an excessive bleeding heart and make excuses all of the time for other people when these individuals make mistakes and failures, which are inexcusable. Believe me, we all make irresponsible mistakes and failures. I plead guilty. Nevertheless, some people simply cannot comprehend things at the pace of others, and some people cannot do things that other people can.

When you do have to criticize your children, keep in mind that they are human and they may have very delicate egos. These egos may be more fragile in the late preteen years as well as the teenage years (Gordon 122-23). Therefore, the pain that they sustain from being susceptible to criticism is more legitimate than you may realize.

"Sticks and stones may break my bones but names will never hurt me."

That is one of the worst proverbs that any parent, teacher, counselor, or mentor can tell a child who is being picked on. For one reason, you basically tell that child to lie and be a hypocrite. That expression is simply not true and everyone knows it. So why do adults tell children that? Everyone has feelings. We all know that name-calling, insults, put downs, sarcasm, condescending remarks, and any mean-spirited teasing can cause pain and tremendous emotional damage. I can certainly attest to that from my experiences.

If you are truly compassionate and understanding of kids being picked on and how their feelings can be easily hurt, then you should be wise enough to put yourself in the position of that child and know very well that they can easily feel pain when they are being put down. They are made of flesh and blood, just like you. We have all had our unfair share of mistreatment in our lives. Ironically, many have more when they're adults.

Perhaps more significantly, kids who use that expression defensively while trying to believe it know that it is untrue and they may feel weak, inferior, or inadequate as a result, especially if their parents tell them to say it. They should never have to feel that way based on a false expression. Never tell people, particularly children, to say it! Amen.

Though this might be difficult in the early stages in a child's life, one of the best things that you can impart to a child, especially when they are moving up through the formative years of school, is to tell them that no one is free or 100% safe from anything in life. This can range from tragically losing a loved one, a parent losing a job, having a horrible accident, or when others simply struggle to make livings, especially if they have families to support.

9/11/01

Though you can't force feed notions on children to be 100% empathic, one suggestion that may help them, might be the September 11th, 2001 attacks on our American soil and the thousands of lives that were lost. The point is that we are all vulnerable and not the least bit invincible, and that calamitous day abundantly exemplifies that. What happened that day ultimately demands the need for compassion, understanding, and empathy for and from anyone and everyone. This is not just to help prevent further terrorist attacks that destroy people and places, but to bless everyone with the wisdom to love everyone, since the attacks have threatened the welfare of our economy and our survival. We all have the need to feel safe and be loved.

Besides feeling safe and loved through compassion, understanding, and empathy, communication must be used in all settings. **Communication** is definitely a key element that is vital to the individuals that you are readily in contact with. Do everything in your power to create support groups to generate the compassion and empathy that you need to build relationships with people. Establish an emotional and personal connection with as many people as you can that you can truly communicate with.

Effort should be valued more than performance. This is particularly true for the students with learning disabilities or anything else that forces one to struggle. When you understand this, you will be more aspired to develop more compassion and empathy for people from all walks of life. If you realize that some persons may not be good at one thing, you will encourage them to look into something else, which might be better.

I do think it is true that when people create problems of their own they blame others who they may depend on to bail them out. Lord knows that these factors can stem from anything such as pregnancies for young girls and women who are unprepared to be mothers, to teenagers committing dastardly deeds, such as petty theft, dealing drugs, vandalism, and so on.

Certainly, when persons get themselves into jams, whether it is their fault or not, they may still need someone to lean on, and find some kind of sounding board from persons who are willing to be compassionate and understanding. Of course, it is impossible for everyone to have a full amount of that on every issue in life. Much of that depends on the fact that certain people are more involved with issues that they are forced to deal with, or they choose to get involved because of a natural interest in them.

Another factor, which is very paramount, is that some individuals can only be so empathic, because they have had little or no exposure to so many things, and they have not been confronted with things that others have been forced to deal with.

As we know, we live in a society that demands that boys and girls behave in ways that fit gender expectations. Boys and men are taught to be bold, strong, self-assured in composure, demeanor, and posture. Quite often, they are not taught to be soft, sensitive, and emotionally vulnerable. They are especially taught to not break down and cry in front of other guys who have more macho personas.

Girls and women are taught to be more docile, submissive, sympathetic, loving, gentle, empathic, and sensitive to anyone and everyone whose around them. That is fine to a point, but why can't boys and men exemplify those qualities too? Sure, boys will be boys, but that doesn't mean they cannot have compassion, understanding, and empathy.

Many men are callous and lack compassion for their wives, especially when they have children. As we know, many women are stereotyped as being subservient and dependent.

I can bet that mothers can feel useful when they teach their children to read, write, figure, and many other things. Later on, after the empty nest, many women tend to feel empty inside, because they may be bored and lonely, and they may not always have people to spend time with. They may want to go back to work again, not just to make extra money, but more importantly, to feel passionate about life and to fully engage with it. I certainly learned this through my experiences.

Personal Empathic Experiences

Empathy is an attribute that has made me become a better person, and it can do wonders for everyone else. I became very empathic of persons who suffer from loneliness, isolation, alienation, and any form of chronic sluggishness, due to being slighted, denied, belittled, or rejected. I could see a part of myself in these individuals.

I became more empathic when I lived in Staunton, Virginia for nearly two years. It was a nice but astoundingly ultra-conservative town that was not much for innovation. I had just graduated from Bethany and I was missing it fiercely. For the first five or six months, I sobbed so many times because I missed my friends so badly and I was away from all of them. They were very much a family to me. I was all alone trying to make friends, and I did manage to make a few, who turned out to be absolutely great.

I managed to meet some girls and have some dates once in a while. I worked in radio because I was pursuing the broadcast field at the time. I worked in the evening more often than the day at the radio station. I did like the area and the town in some ways. I was enthralled by the majestically scenic mountains, the historical landmarks, and the fact that it was in a college belt area.

I lived right down the road from an all women's college. I used to venture up 25 miles to James Madison University in Harrisonburg to meet girls and party with the Sigma Nu brothers. Unfortunately, I was not able to do this very often. I also made pilgrimages to Lexington where Washington & Lee University is, to party with the Sigma Nu's and visit the National Headquarters, because Sigma Nu was founded there at Virginia Military Institute. My father and oldest brother attended Washington & Lee. Some of the ultra conservatism stimulated me to an extent because I have some conservative blood in me. I could get reruns of cop shows that I couldn't get before such as <u>Kojak</u>, <u>The Streets of San Francisco</u>, <u>Charlie's Angels</u>, and <u>The Mod Squad</u>.

Nevertheless, I was very overwhelmed by the area because though many people were friendly and polite, they weren't much for cultivating persons who appeared to be outsiders. It was though their philosophy was "Let outsiders be outsiders." I had some very loving relatives in Harrisonburg who I met for the first time less than three months after I moved to Staunton. They treated me to dinner a few weeks before Thanksgiving and then again on Turkey Day. They were very much the only family that I had there, but I didn't see them as much as I would have liked to. One member of the family told me that I was an outsider in Staunton when I told him that I couldn't help but feel like one.

The isolation and loneliness that I felt helped me develop some compassion in myself. I began to think that I could identify with people who felt left out, denied, rejected, and totally empty inside. I felt this way over half of the time.

There were times when things became so insipid and lackluster at the radio station, I felt very useless, and since I wasn't making any money to begin with, I became more empathic and understanding of people who had to struggle on many levels. It didn't matter whether it was poverty, lack of people to meet or talk to, lack of a social life, lack of family and friends to get together with, feeling financially strapped, or anything else that made me feel stagnant.

Though I liked the radio business within the first year, the solitude of it did catch up with me even though I felt creative with what I did. I spent a great deal of time reading and keeping up with what went on in the world. This really helped me open my mind to many things. My socially deprived and turbulent past enabled me to be more understanding of people who are lonely, feel unloved, and uncared for.

I once had a stomach virus for at least two or three days while I was still living in Staunton. I was living alone and I had just broken off a relationship with a lovely girl who lived in Harrisonburg, which was bleak from the start. I remember trying to watch a Monday night football game that the Steelers were playing, but I laid on the couch vegetating. I couldn't eat, sleep, vomit, or move my bowels because I was incapacitated with stomach gas. I eventually drove myself to the hospital. I had to wait at least an hour for a doctor to come in and treat me.

I almost felt like I was dying because of all of the pain that I was enduring. I began thinking to myself about how elderly people or anyone stricken with painful and terminal illnesses must feel when they are ravaged with pain or anything else that ails them.

I have always been very healthy. I thank God for that. My teeth have always been excellent. Nonetheless, I believe I was becoming more empathic of people who not only suffer on a physical level, but the combination of that with the emotional damage that I sustained in my lonely life, made me empathic of people who may lack medical resources or other environmental outlets that are conducive and vital for them.

I remember a time when I was so empty inside and spiritually inert for an entire month in Staunton. I was not suicidally depressed. In hindsight, I knew that the immediate period that followed Bethany's Alumni weekend was going to be horrendously drab and dull unless I prepared to deal with it before hand.

For seven months, I was anxiously awaiting a one-year reunion of my beloved alma mater. Anyway, I realized when I left Bethany and returned back to Virginia that I enormously alienated my friends and the special times that I spent with them. Just knowing that I had to leave and go back to something so sluggish, hit me like a tidal wave. I had no trouble doing my job efficiently in fact I think that was what helped me with my pain.

I tried as an experiment to go to the park and sit down on a bench; just like many elderly persons or displaced veterans who gaze at the pigeons and all of the children playing and laughing. Many lonely people who engage in this behavior regularly become potentially depressed, because they are bored, lonely, unloved, and they have no way to occupy their time, especially if they feel like they have no one to share their lives with. While doing this, I developed more empathy for these kinds of people because there were chronic periods when I had felt so futile and terribly lonely. My experiences helped me acquire compassion and understanding of others, because I was more willing to be empathic.

We can understand from our past experiences, that everyone needs compassion, understanding, and empathy. When a child is ill and/or has been hurt, we are compassionate enough to treat a child who is in need. The same rule applies to pets and adults, regardless of race, color, religion, gender, age, national origin, veteran status, and disability, like the one that I have.

Counseling services for everyone

We must bestow on our children at a young age, perhaps around 5 or 6 (that could be debatable though) that there is no need to be ashamed of anything that makes them feel sad or angry, especially if it warrants the need for professional mental health services. We know how naturally cruel children can be, especially if they find out that certain students are seeking mental health counseling. They may be picked on and written off as the worst outcasts of all.

So many people are challenged to make themselves happy. Society often labels persons who are in need of services as quackos, mental cases, psychos, weirdoes, losers, freaks, imbeciles, loonies, and the like. It is so amazing. You hear vernacular terms for mental institutions such as nuthouses, funny farms, and even insane asylums seem to carry a negative connotation.

Counseling services from therapists, psychologists, and social workers should be encouraged for anyone without feeling ashamed or stigmatized. Even psychiatry may be a necessary outlet for some and we know that it often is. I certainly have compassion, understanding, and empathy toward people who would feel embarrassed to tell some people, because it is obviously very personal and you have a right to keep it private. Everyone should have the decency to respect that. Nonetheless, no one should feel ashamed of seeking any kind of psychological help.

Unfortunately, I never had any counseling services while I was growing up. Besides having ADD, a profound learning disability, generalized anxiety disorder, and severe periodic bouts of depression, I developed a case of post-traumatic-stress-disorder through the years. This was spawned by many years of constant mental/verbal abuse, ridicule, and humiliation from certain individuals. There was alienation, social deprivation, isolation, profound lack of communication with persons who would have been vital for me, and of course the lack of opportunities and resources to use and develop talents that I didn't know I had until much later.

I did engage in some counseling services at Bethany and when I was in Graduate School. My friends at Bethany provided their own form of counseling by listening to me with compassion and understanding. They sincerely loved me. I had gone to a priest for six years, who was the former chaplain at Bethany. He had been a source of inspiration for me and he remains one.

More significantly though, I have gone to a therapist to help me face my demons in a way to manage and own my emotions rather than them owning me, which they often threaten to do. I suppressed more emotional turmoil than you can imagine. I have benefited immensely, especially when I vented some rage through my therapy sessions. My spirits are raised enormously, and I have felt that I can take greater control of my life, because I am standing on fertile ground with seeds that I have personally planted.

Therapy is a term with many relative meanings. Jogging and any form of exercise can be therapeutic. Working out on a punching bag has been cathartic for me, not to mention getting in good physical shape. Reading is conducive and so is making anything, whether it is a dessert for a party, or painting pictures, or just doing anything that curbs any pathology.

After my grandfather retired from his engineering profession, he actively engaged in gardening and making rugs. I would often marvel over what a fabulous job he had done when I had seen his creations. My grandmother said that those activities were therapy for him. This helped him curb any potential monotony that he could have been forced to endure if he had not occupied his time constructively.

Counseling and Psychological services are a blessing to people who are willing and able to take advantage of them. I used to know someone who told me that he had gone to a psychiatrist when he was a little boy. This was in regard to his parents getting a divorce.

Children suffer terrible distress and traumas in many ways, especially if they are physically battered or even mentally battered like I was. No matter what age or how a person is suffering from any tremendous emotional grief, any form of therapy should be kept with an open mind if not strongly recommended with compassion, understanding, and empathy.

Teaching children to be sensitive to others

Children should also be taught not to tease others who have family members with visible and or well-known weaknesses. Some ways to help is to tell them that there are famous people who had trouble in school and had psychological problems and became very successful. Henry Winkler is dyslexic and we know how intelligent he is. There are many famous people who have had learning difficulties. Albert Einstein had difficulties in school. This gives kids an idea that there is hope for them.

Compassion for strangers

It is natural for people to feel some tension or discomfort when a seemingly displaced, poor person approaches you on the street and asks you for 50 cents for a cup of coffee or to make a phone call. However, even if these persons don't need food right away, they may indeed just want to talk to someone, whether they are in the midst of a crisis or they just want to have some kind of human contact that rejuvenates their souls. It may grieve you sometimes to help someone who is in dire need of something, but keep in mind, you could be in a similar situation or worse one day.

When I was working on my Masters' degree at Marshall University, I was sometimes approached by certain persons when I saw them on the street. I remember a few of them were stunningly audacious in the way that they approached me. The ones that I encountered were overbearing due to their temerity. I feared that if I became too well acquainted with these persons, they would have been calling my number or worse; knocking at my door at ungodly hours. You must realistically concede that there are con artists in the world who strive to deceive others.

I've heard some people say that if poor, destitute people knocked on their doors begging for food, clothing, and shelter, that they would help them without the slightest hesitation, because they would be holding compassion and understanding for these individuals. That sounds like a warm-blooded standpoint, but it is hardly a practical one in many ways without being prudent. These persons could manipulate you into being robbed, brutalized, raped or murdered. It is a fact of life, and no matter how much love you have in your heart, you must acknowledge reality. It is sad but true that you can only have so much pity for some individuals, including yourself.

Self-Pity

We are told that we shouldn't feel sorry for ourselves. "Cut the self-pity"; "quit crying," and whatever else. I have news for people who think that. That's a myth that could not be more false. Why? Because feeling sorry for yourselves is extremely easy to do and everyone is guilty of it. As we get older, we realize that our harshest critics are ourselves. We easily tear ourselves down with intra personal insults. It is good to humble yourself to deter any illogical thoughts of grandeur. However, you can like yourself by having the purest form of conceit. You can be humble and modest; this helps you love yourselves the way you would love others.

If you are lonely, sad, and empty, and need someone to lean on, by all means cry and let it bleed. It makes you more human, loving, and sensitive to others and yourself. Go as far as you can with it if you have to (Ellis 215). I've learned from my experiences that if you have to let out all of that pain by saying horrendously irrational things when you are struggling, it can become a paradox that enables you to understand that futility can become optimism through a personal catharsis. It may be like God is testing you to fear Him by staying alive and rising to the occasion to keep fighting the good fight. I have done that many times in life, and I have ironically improved in many ways as a result.

There is a song by the rock band Styx, entitled "Fooling Yourself (The Angry Young Man)" that strikes a special chord with me. Styx composer, Tommy Shaw, who had written and sung the song, said that he knew that he was writing the song about another individual, then, he realized that he could personally relate to it himself. He implied that it was about having that one unexpected setback that you were not really anticipating. However, you acknowledge that when the going gets tough, the tough get going, and you bounce back and you ultimately succeed. You will understand the meaning if you read and/or listen to the lyrics.

I don't encourage others to beat themselves up with self-pity all of the time, especially on protracted levels, but if it gets to a point when you must purge pent up emotions to cleanse yourself, do so, and shortly remind yourself afterwards that you are unique and special and you deserve to be happy. Tell yourself that you may not be successful at everything that you do and you don't have to be, contrary to what some people may have told you. Then say, "I won't succeed in life if I sit and mope around and do nothing, right?" Absolutely!!

I would like to add that if intimate compassion and understanding doesn't work with one feeling sorry for him or herself, then reverse psychology can be used by saying, "Well if you keep crying or quitting, then, you will be a loser"; "show me some confidence, otherwise you are a loser and you won't get anywhere." That can have marvelous effects on one to get back on his or her feet again. I only recommend that as a last resort if all else doesn't work.

Don't be fooled by thinking that self-pity is for losers and wimps, because everyone has it sometimes, and if they say they do not, they are denying it. You know that you need C, U, and E just like a homeless person needs a warm place to sleep.

One key paradox of being empathic; however, is that you can only put your thoughts and feelings in the position of distinct individuals so much, no matter how much you want to help the individuals. This is because their grief and sufferings are uniquely theirs based on them being unique individuals (Toma and Levey 27).

There are so many people in the world who are complex, and of course, the astronomical population of the world makes us aware that we at times, have more people in the world than we can accommodate. We depend on our president, congressmen, senators, judicial system, and all significant politicians and bureaucrats to create a world of hope and inspiration to all of us who undoubtedly need it. Sure, we know politics is notoriously corrupt. We the people do not want to hear broken promises and empty lies; we've certainly heard plenty of them, but keep in mind, every person on the face of the Earth is corrupt. No one is 100% impeccable.

I have talked to people with significant positions in the corporate world, who have said that when people ascend to important levels of prestige in politics and corporate America, they are more susceptible to having their morals challenged, because they may be forced to make decisions that they would rather not. Some may feel that they have to go against their principles to assess who is valuable and who is expendable. Unfortunately, many end up compromising their virtues. Even if they do nothing legally wrong or even morally wrong in a sense, they may be devoured with guilt regardless.

If you think you are someone who is too soft hearted and does not have a somewhat hardened heart to make downsizing decisions to save money in order to make money, then, you may want to think twice as to how high you want to climb up that company ladder. I think the same principle applies if you are in the military, especially if you have trouble taking what you can dish out.

Compassion and understanding for yourself

One of the most critical factors of all that we must continue to keep in mind is that not one single person can save and help everyone in the world who suffers from everything. You can't realistically believe that getting involved with too many different things at the same time, just so you are living up to your duties as a humanitarian, will ultimately reduce or prevent any potential remorse. You owe it to yourself to be compassionate and understanding of yourself; simply put, you need to take care of yourself. Everyone else must do the same. The more empathic you are of others in that regard, the more you can be sensitive and thoughtful to your own personal needs.

Believe me, I am very much a romantic. I wish the world was comprised of so many benevolent, magical forces that could solve all of our problems to establish peace, love, and joy, so we can all live happily ever after. Sorry!! I am a realist too. I know the real world isn't like that.

At any rate, everyone needs personal time with some good old-fashioned rest and relaxation. Of course, you don't want to alienate your loved ones. However, you owe it to yourselves to be truly happy, and you can do so by being loving, and giving at the same time.

The more you dedicate ample time to a greater good, the better you will feel about yourself, but you must be true to yourself by acknowledging who and what you are. If you don't think realistically about what is best for you, you may deny opportunities and chances in your life that are in front of you without even knowing it.

We all have failures and we all make mistakes. This will always be an infinite factor in life. Some failures and mistakes are preventable and others are not. Quite often, we don't realize our failures and mistakes until much later on. We tend to maintain feelings of guilt over them. I still have regrets over some things that I was thoughtless of. I have learned to put things in perspective by emphatically examining my past and seeing things that could have been helped and things that could not.

I have learned to forgive myself for many of my failures and mistakes and to compensate for them the best way that I can; all of this regards compassion and understanding for myself.

The three factors that I emphasize in this chapter were rarely granted to me while I was growing up. To me, the bottom line is to modify the meaning of the word failure in a way to make it more acceptable and forgivable; this way, it will inspire everyone to never give up. Perhaps the best motto for the C, U, and E chapter should be the more that you fail, the more that you allow yourself to ultimately succeed in the long run.

One proverb to keep in mind is "We have not failed unless we have failed to try." We all have to struggle and fight, and when we maintain compassion and understanding while fighting the good fight, we are more bound to succeed in many things we do, if not everything. If we work hard at hobbies and professions that we love and still remain unsuccessful, our so-called failures may paradoxically put us on the right paths to succeed sometime after we find our niches in life.

When persons with handicaps see empathic qualities of others toward them, they are more inclined to not apologize for their handicaps. More than that, they become more adamant in accepting them and building on them to be the best that they can be.

Elderly people still feel young at heart based on simply being human. Many have managed to start new whole lives for themselves when they retire from their career professions. Their humanness is essentially what motivates them to feel useful at all times, and though there may be physiological deterioration when they age, like everyone else, they are inclined to preserve that motivating force or "internal music note" that fulfills one's spirit to be creative and feel useful. This makes one feel happy because the individual feels a love of his/her own life, which enhances him/her to love others that the individual is around.

There are periods in our lives when we simply may not have the resources to work through things, or we may not have the answers to questions in order to make us more aware.

The main point is that we are merely human and everyone is plagued by these kinds of things.

Everyone has faults, weaknesses, handicaps, and problems that we are sensitive of, and though we may not all have the same kinds, if we at least make an attempt to look deeper into the soul of each person, we will find that we can relate to them, and we will be more destined to transcend with compassion, understanding, and empathy.

Always remember that old adage, "People who live in glass houses should not throw stones." We are all glass house residents.

CHAPTER SEVEN

Courtesy & Respect

If you can understand the concepts from the previous chapter, then you should certainly be able to understand the significance of courtesy and respect for all individuals. This includes kids as well as adults. Of course, children and even adults are too often victimized by a lack of these two essentials. However, if you regularly exercise the concepts of C, U, & E that were emphasized in Chapter 6, you will be more inclined and obligated to extend courtesy and respect to others, and then you will expect the same from them.

The opposites of courtesy and respect are discourtesy and disrespect. On the surface, they do not sound like words with ugly meanings do they? That may be part of the problem. Now if you take words like murder and suicide, they sound very brutal and painful, because you know one regards extreme disrespect for another person's life, and the other is the same toward one's own life. God only knows how many examples there are of discourtesy and disrespect.

Mean spirited teasing comes from discourtesy and disrespect. Poking your nose into another person's business by asking how much money their father makes each year, or asking why their parents are divorced, or whether their parents smoke or not, are samples of showing a lack of respect toward the privacy of others.

We all have curious natures, which are good. However, if we are not careful, they can carry us away. Fortunately, many people have the decency and respect to keep their noses out of the business of others. Sadly, though, people gossip and deliberately pry into other people's business, ranging anywhere from someone reading someone else's mail to the media zeroing in on every minute thing that a prominent person or celebrity does. Simply put, exercise courtesy and respect by keeping your nose out of the business of others.

Non verbal Cues

Nonverbal cues that are discourteous can be very easily detected by people, especially young children. The most seemingly subtle nonverbal cues can constitute a lack of courtesy and respect. For example, mocking and snickering side way glances at one who makes mistakes in front of a group of people. Other examples would be glaring at someone or staring at someone to deliberately irritate them. Even condescendingly staring at someone, as though you are analyzing or scrutinizing that person as a second-class citizen, represents a lack of courtesy and respect.

There may be no Dick and Jane way of teaching children etiquette to be 100% courteous, because we know that we may have to remind them over and over again until they become more consistent on an adequate level. Of course, that may depend on each child.

Some kids are obedient, well behaved, and docile, even though they threaten to be more rebellious and willful during their teen years when they are developing identities for themselves. We know that there are others who are mean, arrogant, obnoxious, and are always creating trouble. We don't always know why that is. It could be from genetic and/ or environmental factors. We all eventually learn that you can't program kids to be totally courteous at all times. Some do try though. Again, keep in mind that we must allow kids to falter, then, they can compensate from the lessons that they learn.

I may be at a disadvantage since I am not a parent, but I have learned from my experiences and what I have observed in others, that people respect themselves more when they do good things for others. The more that they are accustomed to doing so on a regular basis, the more they adhere to those principles, the same way they do when they are taught to flush the toilet after they use it, or when they wash their hands.

One thing that is for sure, principles of courtesy may be instilled upon children at young ages, but they are not really developed until they sufficiently practice them and put them into day-to-day use. Respect from others, and one's self is earned by what you say, do, and think. They don't just magically learn it all out of the clear blue sky. It takes time and practice.

I definitely believe in teaching kids to politely ask for things by saying "May I have some of that please?" I also believe they should ask their parents to be excused from the dinner table. Teaching your children to bring their dishes and plates to the kitchen sink are invaluable ways to teach them to be respectful of their parents, because they learn to cooperate with them and obey them.

Principles of courtesy should definitely be taught by emphasizing that you should ask "May I and please?" Other examples are "Would you please pass the salt and pepper?" Other examples are "May I please be excused from the dinner table"; and saying "no thank you" when you are offered something is certainly a sample of courtesy and respect if you say it in a kind and polite tone of voice. Children should not only be taught these factors for the mere principle to respect their parents; they should be taught this to cooperate on a daily regular basis with their family members and others that they are in contact with in and outside of the home.

From my experiences, it seems that courtesy is not consistently practiced until people grow up to a certain point in their lives. That is understandable and natural, but that does not excuse parents, teachers, and adults of not teaching kids manners at a young age. We know that kids will not always be polite, and I know that can be very embarrassing to parents and older siblings. Nevertheless, all of that goes with the territory when the kids are growing up, so it really takes time.

However, when you do have to intervene, it is crucial that you approach them in a way that does not make them feel inadequate and inferior. For example, if a child's manners at the dinner table (between the ages of 4 and 12) are sloppy at times, such as smacking lips or not always using utensils properly, they should be consulted with in a courteous and respectful tone without viciously reprimanding them; the latter only embitters the child and it may not dissuade the child from doing it again. Mind you, I know this is not always easy to do, because children can and do test you, but you must keep that theory in mind no matter what.

There are no definitive answers and methods that will produce ideal outcomes. However, there are some approaches that help. Some of them are listed below.

- *"It does not look or sound good when you do that"*
- *"I know you are still just a kid and even adults can be sloppy and remiss at times, but you need to be more conscientious about those things"*
- *"Now you know better than that"*
- *"Now you are a smart kid"*
- *I know you get discouraged at times when you have to work so hard and I know you may have to make little notes to remind yourself which is fine, but you must keep working at it and never give up."*

Teaching children at a young age that it is important to hold the door open for others is very significant. I think the sooner that you teach children to say "excuse me" after they sneeze, or to say "thank you" when something is given to them or when someone does something nice for them, or to say "sorry" whenever they may accidentally bump into someone, the more inclined they will be to consistently exercise courtesy and respect.

Who's to say what is the best way to teach all children the mores of courtesy and respect, especially, since some kids don't understand concepts as early as others might? Certainly, parents and teachers can't afford to worry about every form of behavior of every child all of the time. Nevertheless, the sooner you attempt to instill these values in them, and the more often you remind them to consistently practice them, the chances are better that they will do so if you teach them in civil, kind, and nurturing ways that encourage their willingness to use these qualities on a regular basis.

I think the best way to do so is to reward them by telling them how well they are doing when they demonstrate that they are doing so. Tell them how much you love them and that you are proud of them.

You do not have to shower them with accolades every time that they are kind and respectful. Kids can get annoyed with that, even at a very young age.

I don't believe rewarding your kids with money, for being courteous and respectful, is an intelligent tactic. In a way, you could be bargaining for one's expected behavior through dollars. As a result, kids could be doing nice things for people and behaving well only for the financial principle instead of the humanistic one. Not only can that make children greedy, they may only intend to be courteous and respectful at times when they anticipate overt rewards (especially money). We must cultivate habits of exercising courtesy and respect the best that we can by being tactful and discreet. Of course, no one is perfect, because we certainly are at error at times, even in these regards.

Tact is certainly an essential component for everyone to use for people to get along easier. Businesses would not thrive very well and social life would revert to the utter most stone-age crudeness, if persons were not the least bit trained in the school of using tact. Tact means quick awareness of the feelings of others and consideration for them.

Insincerity can often be a drawback when one is being tactful in order to prevent hurting the feelings of others. People are often hurt when others are not tactful and discreet with them. Tactless people simply don't stop and think. There are persons who are so candidly insolent that their minds and verbal behaviors seem to be drawn by a magnet, so to speak. Being tactful which helps generate courtesy and respect is imperative to all of us. It makes no difference.

Positive regard is referred to as respect. This regards the ability to appreciate an individual as someone who is dignified and full of worthiness. It makes no difference of one's external factors, such as one's behavior, demeanor, appearance, and so on. To show positive regard or respect is to express appreciation of a person as being unique, worthy, and special (Rogers 307).

Respect for Children and Teenagers

Children are too often treated with such a lack of courtesy and respect, especially teenagers. God knows that I can testify to that with my harrowing memories. Parents and adults should never belittle their children with name-calling, put-downs, blatant insults, and especially insults to their intelligence when they are really growing up between the ages of 11 and 18. Even after that, kids, or should I say very young adults, are often talked down to like they are naïve, ignorant imbeciles, who have minimal knowledge or none whatsoever. Too often, kids are patronized, and they feel offended when adults or older siblings constantly talk down to them. Certainly, you can't expect them to behave like much older kids or full-grown adults when they simply have not grown into them yet (Gordon 122-23).

Now, we all know that children need guidance and discipline, and you must use constructive criticism instead of destructive criticism. We all lose our tempers, which is natural. Kids can and will test you, especially if they knowingly disobey you or anyone else that may be an important figure in their lives.

I realize kids don't understand the concepts of courtesy and respect as well as ones who are well into their teens (but even some of those don't seem to). However, they can tell even at an age as young as 4 or 5, when they are being conned or lied to, and when they do, they become willful and defiant, because they rightfully resent what they know is an injustice to them. This would be insulting the intelligence of a child.

I am not a parent, but I think that I can empathize fairly enough to understand that parents may have preconceived notions of their children being so little and innocent, even well beyond those years when they lose so much of their innocence.

I certainly cannot create an absolute criteria on how to be 100% courteous and respectful with teenagers when you must communicate with them. We know that teenagers grow to become more independent, because they are growing up to become unique individuals with exclusive identities.

Teenagers become rabidly dependent on their friends and peers. They become rebellious, sassy, and in some cases, intractable if not impossible to live with. Nonetheless, it is imperative for all parents to backtrack to their teenage years when they were going through changes and the times when they had difficulty adjusting to them. It is a terribly difficult period in the teenagers lives when they are developing identities for themselves and they are trying to see what is best for them.

They also are trying to find who their real friends are or if the friends they hang out with, are real ones that they can count on and trust.

I know that many kids can be cocky. Some think they know it all and they can seem like a pain when they are unwilling to cooperate and help out, because they want to have fun and have a good time. Certainly, that can disgruntle any parent, but keep in mind that all kids, especially teenagers live in the present moment. The here and now is so imperative to them. Some teenagers may not realize how foolish and insignificant the things that they are doing really are until much later on. More so, they are actually much more sensitive about delicate issues that are very personal to them, especially the opposite sex.

The sex factor is extremely crucial for parents to understand, especially because their kids are being more exposed to different ideas and problems that boys and girls typically have in relationships. Things are so new to them and they are often insecure in how to deal with them, not just because of how unsure that they may be of the people they are involved with, but the friends and people that they interact with may create problems for them as well. Some kids don't know who they are compatible with and they may never be around the individuals who they could be compatible with. This was a major obstacle for me.

I was constantly mistreated by persons who had no respect for my taste in music. Not only was I taunted by some of my peers and so-called friends, but there were college educated people in their early 20's and well beyond, who had shown me a massive lack of respect. They did not consider for one moment that I had a right to my opinions, and even more so, they were not the least bit empathic as to why I liked my music. They also did not even try to understand that it made me feel special and it was a profound expression of who and what I was and still am.

I have inferred that these behaviors from these supposedly educated individuals were due to being shallow, pigheaded, inconsiderate, and too immature to be respectful of me. More than that, they simply weren't willing to open their minds. No matter how you look at it, there is no excuse for an unwillingness to keep an open mind, let alone, to be discourteous and disrespectful of others.

Kids and especially teenagers have strong opinions regarding their musical interests and politics. These aspects can be very indicative of their unique identities. They are bent on expressing them with pride on very conspicuous levels. Political opinions of sub-teens and teenagers can have a great deal of validity to them. Parents and adults will not always agree with them, but do all politicians agree with each other to begin with? Why do you think there is so much frustration in the ostensible unsuccessful attempt to create bipartisanship on all levels, especially in our American government?

If parents and adults respect their kids in a way that makes them feel intelligent and old enough to have their opinions, which they are definitely entitled to, they will feel respected and they may be more inspired to grant others with the same courtesy and respect (Gordon 122).

If the opinions of your children are inconsistent with yours, it is crucial that you respect that they have the right to their opinions; just as you do. They will respect you even more if you grant them the respect that they deserve. If you denounce them when you disagree with them or vehemently criticize something or someone that is special to them, they could and often do become bitter, resentful, and spiteful.

Always remember that children have the ability to develop individual opinions. Though they may not be fully grown up yet, does not mean there is no legitimate independent intelligence on the child's part (Gordon 122).

Just because your child should listen to you, doesn't mean you should not listen to your child. Moreover, don't tell your child what opinions you think he/she should have (122). This patronizing behavior is wrong (122).

Don't talk down to your child like he/she is too ignorant about so many things, especially when they are adolescents filled with infatuation. All individuals are critical enough of themselves at any age (123).

Encourage your children to be the best they can be but unconditionally accept them for what they are. Kids don't need to feel inadequate when you try to make your kids do things where there is a lack of interest or no talent. It is bad enough to try to make a child do something that he/she doesn't want to do, let alone be unable to do it (123).

If you think that you should consult with your kids in order for them to exemplify more etiquette qualities, then, a way to do so might be "I know you are old enough and smart enough to be more courteous, so not to insult your intelligence, but please be more thoughtful about it from now on and in the long run, you'll benefit more. I know you can do it." That is better than saying: "Make sure you hold the door open for the girl" (using condescending tone).

It is very bad to pick on kids when they are well into their teens. This is when they are growing to be more independent. It is paramount that teenagers develop self-esteem levels that make them psychologically healthy. When kids are belittled and humiliated during their teen years (especially high school years) and well into their adult years, the more they are bound to sustain drastic emotional throes. This is because they are growing up to be unique individuals, and if they are badly mistreated during these years, their self-esteems are dreadfully lowered. This can scar them for life.

Naturally and rightfully, kids resent being mistreated because they know very well that they should be treated with the courtesy and respect that they deserve. They know that being treated otherwise is a major injustice that they do not deserve.

Never tell a child that he/she should never masturbate. Never classify that as something that should never be discussed or even thought about (Gordon 105-06).

Never pound on a family member for information to find out what is wrong. When kids need time alone to think about some things, or they would rather talk to someone else whom they feel more comfortable with, let them do so. If you want your kids to earn respect for themselves, you must give them some independence to find out who they are and what they should be (Dyer 192-93).

Kids should not be taught to feel guilty for their emotional independence. Parents, siblings, and others should try not to pry and make demands to know things like "who were you talking to on the phone" or reading someone's journal to find out personal things, such as relations with the opposite sex. No family members have the right to do that just because they are family members. You might as well eavesdrop on the telephone. It is the same difference. Parents will respect themselves more if they are courteous and respectful of their kids.

Respect for girls and women

Girls and women should always be treated with courtesy and respect. Their loving, gentle, sensitive, compassionate, understanding nature is so vital to everyone in the world. Being housewives and mothers is not all that they may be meant to be. Some are not meant to be either one. Their humanness and their unique individualities compel them to engage with life; just like boys and men.

Regarding their unique personalities, they are not all alike in demeanor, interests, philosophy of life, and the way they interact with people socially, professionally, and intimately.

Women are wrongly perceived as being subordinate to men. Many women are fiercely independent because they are resourceful, self-sufficient, and they are talented in most, if not all areas. There are women who are bold and don't condone any nonsense and they hold nothing back when something is on their minds. When they do this that is all of the more reason to respect them - as long as it is obvious that they are being fair and reasonable and they make you understand something from an ethical standpoint.

Their natural maternal kindness, sensitivities, and inner and outer beauties, are just some of their attributes that they have that should compel everyone to be courteous and respectful of them. I know you have heard this all before, but women are not objects to be solely perceived and used for casual sex. Sure, we all have those lustful cravings for hot, steamy sex whether everyone engages in it or not. Nonetheless, they are human unique individuals and they should always be treated with respect.

They are people too. They cuss, they smoke, they talk about sex, and they can be aggressive at times when they need to be. They are people who are smart enough to have opinions and to think and live independently for themselves. It is too bad that it was not until the 1970's, when they were finally able to convince many others that they have much more to be reckoned with. Even, today, they are discriminated against in the job market for promotions, job openings, and many other things. That is unfair to them and they do not deserve it. They should never be treated like servants or nobodies.

Respect your elders

Regardless of whether some of your elders are easy to get along with or not, or if they are perfectly healthy for their ages, you must show courtesy and respect to them in particular. They may need your help more than anyone else. They also have the knowledge and wisdom to educate you about anything in life, so don't think that once you've grown up to be an adult, you don't have to listen to them anymore. You may need to do so more than you really know.

One thing that I have learned from the elderly is that though it is thoughtful and noble to help them do things that require major or even minor physical energy, some may insist that they can do it themselves, then demonstrate it. If they do so, still always offer to help, even if you know they won't exert any inordinate strain on themselves.

Be thoughtful and considerate, but if they adamantly insist they can do some things when you know they can without getting hurt, let them. Though your intentions may be good, you may offend them by insinuating that they are helpless. Be alert and scrupulous at all times and be assertive with them when you know you have to be.

The main point is, respect the fact that your elders are very much human and they want to feel independent and useful. Therefore, we should all help them to be so with reason and mercy.

Demeaning remarks and labels to elderly people are uncalled for. Listed below are examples.

- *"Move it you old fogie"*
- *Calling a stranger Grandma or Grandpa in a mocking, derisive manner*
- *"Look at all these old dinosaurs singing, dancing, playing ball"*
- *"I didn't know they had gasoline back then" when an elderly person might be complaining about high gas prices.*

Any statements that suggest senility or being "over the hill" are unacceptable when many can efficiently produce when given the opportunities to prove it.

One example that I recall from my school experience regarded a teacher well into his 50's, who seemed rather passive and unresponsive at times. Some students jeered that he was senile, which he most certainly was not. He was a very nice man who didn't deserve such a cruel insult. I remember a person at least four years older, telling us how terribly disrespectful that was, not just because he wasn't senile, but also because it was wrong to begin with. He really underscored the term: "disrespectful." I think some of the students shrugged it off and laughed saying "who cares" and "whatever." That is such typical jargon and behavior from self-centered ingrates during their preteen and teen years. Some kids might have tried to justify their insults by saying "I don't think he is really senile" or "I was just kidding." That may be so, but that does not excuse making mean, disrespectful remarks, especially when he was a very nice man to begin with. Absolutely not!! Kids and even young and middle aged adults can rationalize by saying, "well that will probably never happen to me." Well, I'm sorry. It very well could.

If people are wary about getting AIDS, or anything else that may frighten them, then, they should consider the possibility of being stricken with Alzheimer's Disease. No matter what, you must respect your elders. After all, if you live long enough, you could be like them one day.

Respect for celebrities

You hear excuses like: "Well, celebrities are an exception when it comes to respecting their privacies, because they are famous as opposed to private citizens." Celebrities are equally human as private individuals, so they ought to be entitled to keep their personal lives to themselves without someone making demands; just so some pesky reporters can get a hot scoop in the newspaper or on television to earn a bonus.

We all can't help but be somewhat stimulated by human-interest stories to a degree. It is all part of the nature of the beast. Nevertheless, who cares if Britney Spears said the f word, not knowing that the microphone was on, or if some hot shot pro football player received a speeding ticket? That is their business and the world does not need to know those things.

I think it would be nice if people would come to the realization that any celebrity prominence of individuals does not discredit the fact that they are human beings. They have feelings and they have weaknesses that they are sensitive about; just like all of the rest of us. Why can't we all extend the same respect to them that we would expect for us?

If you try to become empathic of celebrities, maybe you will find that they should be treated with courtesy and respect. If you had the opportunity to know any of them personally, you would probably understand it more than you can imagine. Now, if it is obvious that a celebrity is willing to share things with the public and media, that is one thing, but I think it is important to give them some breathing space too. They are entitled to that, believe it or not. Treat them with respect so they can live as peacefully as they can.

Just because some people may dislike certain celebrities with or without justification, does not give the media and public a moral right to crucify them, which they often do.

I have understood that celebrities feel they have an obligation to respect their fans and to never disappoint them. Some of that may be indoctrinated from their publicists, agents, and some others, but that does not mean that they are obligated to live out the fantasies of their fans by complying with the auras that they convey, then, sacrifice their own lives in the process. More so, the demands that fans place on their idols can overwhelm the celebrities with so much stress, anxiety, and psychological damage. Those are reportedly some of the reasons why many self-destruct.

Celebrities can be drastically crucified by their own images, because they may be astronomically amplified in a way that their images are what solely make them who and what they are. One's celebrity stature is only part of one's life. Believe it or not, it is only a secondary part. They want to be happy and free to be all of who they really are; just like everyone else.

A shining, though, somewhat subtle example of how larger than life images of celebrities can overwhelm the celebrities themselves, comes from the Orson Welles classic film, <u>Citizen Kane</u>. When Charles Foster Kane is running for governor with a gigantic banner hovering over him, it denotes that his persona is threatening to overpower his actual personhood. He poses with his arm up during his speech, apparently symbolizing how Jesus was crucified on the cross, the same way Kane is slowly but surely being crucified as he climbs up the political ladder. The potential for Kane to descend dramatically becomes more possible when his external salience threatens to overwhelm his inner self. In other words, the bigger he becomes, the harder he will fall (Giannetti 420).

I think problems are derived from people demanding that prominent individuals be something more than what they are, without thinking that all individuals need to be themselves in a healthy way. In other words, people are not extending enough courtesy and respect to individuals who are unique in nature, and celebrity statuses do not fully make up the high profile individuals' unique personalities.

I read somewhere that many persons conceal their zaniness or true inner skills behind the images of resplendent celebrities, and the paradox is that they become internally insignificant by compromising their identities, but they also become more bold on the outside. That is astounding yet tragically ironic (Giuliano 86).

I have understood that many celebrities have been victimized by selling themselves out drastically. Well, they should never have to do that. They should never be coerced to behave according to the standards of others who merely accept and respect them the way they want them to be rather than accepting them for who and what they are. Celebrities will tell you that fame and fortune are not everything that they are cracked up to be. Listen to them. If you respect them as celebrities, then you should also respect them as individual human beings. If you see them with their families in public, leave them alone. As I say, let them live.

Self Respect

I mentioned that self-respect is earned rather than given. Certainly, we all feel good when people help us improve on things that we are working on. Having people to lean on inspires us to flourish. I have learned that if we keep plugging away at things that we like to do or at things that we need to do, our self-esteems will blossom in many ways, if we work at things independently. We also earn self-respect by independent decisions that we make through our relations with friends and the opposite sex when we express our convictions adamantly.

No one owes anyone friendship. People become friends with others because they simply want to, and they have rights to make those choices. If you want others to respect you, the least you can do is respect that they are unique individuals who may not always see things your way. If you are wise enough to understand this, you will accept it and respect them for who and what they are rather than demand that they do and be something according to what you want. Subsequently, you will respect yourself more through this practice mainly because you have respect for yourself from the start (Dyer 63). This will be further enhanced if you do anything and everything that you can to do what you know to be right.

Many places and persons engender disrespect and negativity, crippling their family members, teachers, students, and employees when there is little or no cooperation. I, along with many others were victimized by this when I attended an all male prep school for seven years. You have no idea how many busybodies and mean spirited kids and teachers there were that I was forced to deal with. It was a brutal, shallow, competitive environment to begin with, showing little regard for cooperation. However, I have been told that some people are actively trying to change things about the school to make it a more cooperative learning institution. That would be such a miraculous blessing. We should hope and pray for the best.

There were some good teachers who did everything they thought they could to respect the dignity of each person, and they tried not to condone any mistreatment of others. I can bet that there are some that are there now.

My English teacher from my freshman year just might have been the quintessential gentleman and teacher. He would encourage students when they would do well and he would confer with them in respectful yet firm ways when students were not doing so well, even when he knew some of them were slacking. He had never shown favoritism like some certainly did, and if he had any favorites, he kept them to himself, and he always tried to be fair, even though he was rigid and strict.

Unfortunately, I can't say the same for some of the others. The politics of some of the teachers' methods were quite appalling. Going back to the 6th grade, which was my first year at this school, there was a boarding student in my class who was constantly picked on by one particular teacher.

He was disorganized and he was having a hard time adapting to the school and being away from home. I remember the teacher roaring at him that he was the biggest juvenile jackass in the class and he called him a stupid ox.

Another time, this teacher started making fun of this student's yellow shirt in class, which of course inspired the rest of the kids to ridicule him inside and outside of the classroom. I had trouble getting along with this student in many ways because he shot off his mouth at people, just like the way people picked on him. Nevertheless, this student was getting a raw deal from this teacher and his peers.

This teacher would often tell us that if we were puzzled and needed help, come and see him. Well, when students are bullied and degraded by teachers, it does not do much to inspire them to learn and do well in school, in fact it does inhibit them (Jones 125). This can cause a pupil's academic performance to falter drastically.

Many times, this teacher sadistically abused other students on a verbal level. Besides his utter ignorance of persons who were academically challenged and his wrongful blame of them for that, he may have tried to justify his cruel methods by saying, "That's how I was trained" or "That is what I am accustomed to."

One time, this teacher royally humiliated another boarding student by taping his class work on the blackboard for everyone to see it. It was ambiguous, incomplete, and wrong. The teacher then wrote down "Win a prize, what is it?" Does this kind of castigation and derision, constitute courtesy and respect? Does it have anything to do with compassion and understanding? These are rhetorical questions, of course.

There were other teachers in the prep school that I attended, who mortified students with derogatory names, labels, put downs, insults, and sarcastic and condescending gestures and remarks.

Examples range from one teacher who maliciously picked on students all of the time. One time, he made fun of an overweight student by pointing out to a corpulent stranger on the street saying, "There's your brother!" All of the students laughed hysterically.

This same teacher would scoff at certain students in front of groups of others (especially with the big shot jocks being present). He would imitate the way some would walk, talk, and anything else; just for the mere sake of making fun of them.

Another teacher and football coach made fun of a timid student during football practice when they were practicing on a sled. He said to this kid "Pretend that's: Name of bully; he picked on you and everything." The coach probably would have claimed that he was doing so on a positive reinforcing level, to motivate the player to be more aggressive. Well, if so, he was still talking down to this kid, because he perceived him to be less socially adequate in contrast with his peers. This same teacher even read off a list of who was deficient in certain classes in front of the entire class. He said who was deficient in what and he really reprimanded one student who was supposedly failing half of the fundamental classes.

Don't let the politics of any school institution fool you, especially private schools. Deficiency reports should not be punctuated with such degrading negative reinforcement, which does not enhance the possibility of them redeeming themselves on a long-term performance level, even if they make fleeting short-term progress. If they were to practice what they preach in regard to courtesy and respect, then those reports for each individual should be made available only to the students' parents, advisor, headmaster/principal, and the dean of the upper or lower school. Outside those parties, it is none of anyone else's business!!

I witnessed several forms of physical abuse by teachers in this school. I saw one teacher kick a student four times in a row, while ruthlessly and rhetorically asking him "Did I ask for your opinion?!?" He might as well have told him "If I want your opinion, I will give it to you." Those methods of discipline are a disgrace and they may embitter a student to be more rebellious, defiant, and vindictive in the long run, on very extreme levels. It in no way enhances students to be respectful of others, especially if the kid is an outcast who keeps getting dumped on. Kids and even teachers model from these behaviors, and then they become very much a norm, which they certainly were at this school.

There was one particularly preposterous moment regarding a meeting with a key authority figure of the entire lower school when I was in the 7th grade. He expressed his dismay of all of the sarcasm and criticism that he had seen and heard, and he told us to cool it and that no one was perfect. That was all he said. There was never another meeting after that, and nothing had changed. If that was all he was going to say or do, what would have been the point of having the meeting in the first place?

I think it would be great if all schools formulated and incorporated a temporary class during an activities period to teach the significance of courtesy and respect to kids during the J.R. high stage of a student's life. Some role-play could be implemented to inspire students to be more empathic of others feelings, especially when they are becoming teenagers and they are really beginning to formulate their personal identities.

These classes should have very cooperative modalities to them, which encourage the students to express their thoughts and feelings. The teachers should not condone any teasing whatsoever or anything else that would disrupt the class.

Any teacher can testify that it only takes one rotten apple to spoil an entire barrel. It cheats other students of their opportunities to learn and whether they know it or not, students who instigate, cheat themselves as well as the teacher who is trying to teach them.

Nevertheless, the same abuse/derision went on and on, and I had some terribly painful personal experiences during those harrowing seven years. I sustained massive psychological damage, which has scarred me for life.

One time, a teacher belittled me when we were supposed to take some boxes of books to the school store, but sometimes books were taken directly to the classrooms. Anyway, I asked to clarify if we were taking them to the school store and he replied: "Yeah, I think that would be a good idea" (using a sarcastic and mocking tone). All he had to do was courteously say yes because there is nothing wrong with clarifying something. Another incident regarded a time when I was sharpening my pencil in a classroom, and this same teacher rudely snapped, "Quit it Man, I'm Talking!!!" All he had to do was politely say "Would you please hurry up and finish because you're making noise when you do that?"

Isn't it astounding, how political power can slowly but surely corrupt anyone in a particular domain when there are such disturbing influences? Any fool should be able to see that physical abuse and mental abuse are wrong and uncalled for, even if it is not as severe as domestic incidents behind closed doors of families.

CHAPTER EIGHT

Mental Abuse
& Criticism

So many people in this world fail to realize that mental and verbal abuse can be as damaging to a person as physical abuse. Contrary to what some may think, verbal abuse is not just name-calling, like morons, geeks, losers, degenerates, cretins, or any other derogatory labels. Examples of put downs and insults are "your grades are the worst in the school"; "can't you do anything right"; "you're so pathetic and worthless"; "you always make a mess"; "you are the slowest person I have ever known"; "come on and get your head out of your rear"; "quit walking around in a daze"; "you better start thinking," etc. These words can be as psychologically damaging as physical blows.

Being verbally battered can and often does wound someone permanently, because the scars are internalized. Being berated during petty crises and even major crises can constitute mental abuse. This is even more valid if you are being bawled out by pathological rageaholics, who have short, loud, explosive tempers.

Sarcastic remarks at any age, by any aggressor, are samples of abuse if they are purported in painfully obvious discourteous and disrespectful ways.

One of the worst things that can happen to people is to be taunted by peers in utterly childish ways. This can range from playing immature pranks on people, to calling out a person's name, and when that person turns around, the caller turns away pretending he/she had not called at all. Even high schoolers do this, and it is utterly pathetic. I experienced this during my high school years.

People, who are disrespectful of others, can't take what they dish out. It is not because they won't, they simply can't. Threatening people with violence is a sample of mental abuse, even if the aggressor does not really mean it. These people seem arrogant on the surface, but underneath, their self-esteems are quite low and they are very insecure. That is why they are defensive when they are insulted. Persons who are guilty of any discourtesy and disrespect, such as rudeness to family, colleagues, and others, cannot take the heat when someone does the same to them.

One of my false friends told me during my senior year that I should get a lip transplant. I didn't like what he said because I knew he didn't respect me. He also couldn't take what he could dish out. He proved this point many times, especially when people made fun of him about his cheeks.

Patronizing behavior

What is arguably the most subtle form of verbal abuse or discourtesy, is condescending to someone. It may depend on your point of view, but talking down to someone even if you are trying to sound nice, can be very offensive. It can stem from insulting one's intelligence, such as "You shouldn't believe everything that you read" or "Don't bother that person that you were talking to." It could even be "How is it going man? Are you still listening to that rock station that plays some great tunes?" (mocking tone). That is a direct, repetitive experience from a false friend from my senior year in high school. Even walking up to people and slapping people on their backs in pretentiously friendly fashions can be condescending gestures that most people resent because it conveys a lack of courtesy and respect. I had seen how one particular authority figure at the prep school that I attended, would patronize his colleagues. I remember thinking that was very wrong. No one should feel obligated to tolerate any disrespect and mistreatment.

Life is too short

There comes a time when people who are mistreated or mentally abused, can only endure so much. They realize that life is too short. When people are very young, they may rationalize by saying, "Well since I sustained all of this grief when I was a kid, I can bear it even more in the long run, besides, it will only make me stronger." If you become stronger, it is only because you become wiser about how terribly painful it is. That does not mean that you become immune or desensitized to it. We all have feelings. Your humanness and unique individuality tells you that you are special in your own way and you deserve to be treated with respect. That motivates one to grab the snake by the neck and say "no more of this abuse!" "I've had more than my fill and I am not taking it anymore!!!"

People who compulsively afflict emotional damage on others should seek some kind of professional help. Some may need to seek counseling, therapy, or psychiatry. I hope anyone reading this book who is verbally abusive or pathologically rude to others will keep an open mind about it.

You should care for the welfare of others the same way you value your own. If you do, please think very carefully about this, because you may never realize how much pain you may be causing another person until it is too late. Think about it.

Constructive Criticism

Being critical of a person in a way that changes his/her behavior in a desirable direction, without causing resentment and hard feelings can be very difficult (Cawood 43). Some persons such as school teachers, parents, older siblings, and supervisors think they understand the difference between constructive criticism and destructive criticism.

Some people may think that the latter is much the same as the former, because it is criticism, and criticism feels like a put down no matter what.

There are many ways to prevent being destructively critical. There may be more ways of being constructively critical than you think.

Don't insult people when you are angry and frustrated, because that increases the chances of the recipient being angry and defiant. When you realize that you need to confer with someone that you may be angry with, think about your "tone of voice" when you are "angry," impatient, "sarcastic," or venomously "sneering" (Deutsch 31). It is also crucial to be conscientious about general put downs like, "you're pathetic"; "you're always late"; "you're so lazy"; you're in a dream world"; "your attitude is bad." These insults and generalities can cause a great deal of more harm than help (Cawood 43-45).

A "me against you" atmosphere is not a healthy mentality. It should be the individuals involved trying to solve a particular problem. Never tell someone that they never pay attention because they very well may not listen in the long run through feelings of resentment and vengeance (Martin and Osborne 390).

Though many of us including myself can be unintentionally guilty of this, I know that punishing others critically can make another person more resentful if you do it for the sake of getting even with that person. That should not be emphasized as a policy, even though it is easy to do and sometimes difficult to avoid.

It is best to use constructive criticism when you and the recipient are at ease and chilled out. Of course, there are times when you may have to deal with someone on a critical level immediately. If so, try to be aware of your verbal and nonverbal cues that can be so easily detected by the recipient (Cawood 43-45). You would be amazed at how acute the feelings are that many people have, when picking up the most remote and subtle cues that are suggestive of mockery and derision.

When facilitating constructive criticism, keep everything to the point, plus, make it brief (Deutsch 31). Never go on tangents like "Now how did you do on that other assignment" or "How did you perform in that area." Believe me, you could be sowing the seeds of a breeding ground that prolongs bitterness, resentment, and hatred from any recipient.

Ending on a kind word helps positively reinforce the recipient whose morale may go up to improve and/or correct any problems. It is important to listen to everyone's points of view, whether you sense that you will disagree or that you actually know that you do disagree. If so, something appropriate to say would be "I can see that we can't seem to agree so let's see if we can establish a compromise." Be willing to compromise as well as be verbally courteous and polite (Martin and Osborne 391).

Nonverbal cues, suggesting a confrontation, are easily sensed. Examples range from giving dirty looks and looking angry while holding your sides (391). These are body language signals that everyone should be scrupulous of. We all receive forms of criticism, and, sadly, they can be more negatively reinforced than positively. Negative reinforcement may only induce improved performance on short-term levels, while the opposite may produce better performance on long-term levels.

Try to be calm and not testy when you are being constructively criticized. Mind you, we all have our limits. I have had my share of being tested to the limit. Communicate in diplomatic fashions while maintaining strong eye contact and thinking of alternative ways of dealing with problems. Whenever you fight fire with fire, it only brings you down to the level of the person who is being nasty to you. These factors easily lead to what is called "becoming what you hate." In other words, the more you attack others, the more you attack yourself, and you become self-abhorrent.

You've heard the expression "kill with kindness" by making disarming statements such as "I like your sweater" or "You played well in the game" (Martin and Osborne 393). I have reservations about these types of statements because though you may feel compelled to compliment persons who are difficult, it is manipulative behavior that is not necessarily honest, especially if you are disgruntled by one's acrimony toward you. To me, it is best to be up front about unjustified criticism, only approach it the best that you can by being civil, polite, tactful, and discreet with some C & R.

Sometimes accepting destructive criticism is good in hindsight because it makes you wiser and stronger. It gives you something to contrast it with; therefore, you become determined to use and receive positive reinforcement and constructive criticism rather than negative reinforcement and destructive criticism.

This leads me to what some might consider a controversial issue of how you can kid around with your family and friends about some things, and still remain courteous and respectful. Again there are no universal maxims that befit everyone, but there are certainly some ideas and principles to keep in mind that may help.

Friction in Relationships

Friction can ironically preserve relationships because it challenges you to be flexible and make compromises. People know that people must work together cooperatively to make relationships strong and thriving. That means being willing to compromise based on acknowledging what responsibilities you have to preserve your relationships, more so, treat everyone with the courtesy and respect that they rightly deserve, since they are unique individuals to begin with, let alone human beings (Duncan and Rock 46-51, 86, 95).

However, sometimes, people become so close that they allow more friction than they should. That all goes with the territory. Persons should stop and think in particular cases as to what seems questionable, then communicate as to what is wrong and think in terms of people against a difficult situation rather than emphasizing the problem as a good guy vs. bad guy scenario (Deutsch 30-32).

Relationships fail not always because they could be wrong from the start, but also because most people do not want to correct their problems. Everyone wants his/her own way, which can undermine the principles being underscored in this chapter and the previous one.

Affectionate Insults

No matter what, you should develop more expansive tolerances for affectionate insults from true friends and anyone else who cares for you and respects you. We are all guilty of crossing the line sometimes when we say things instinctively that we really should not say. If so, think about what you have said, apologize, and try not to let it happen again.

A fraternity brother of mine, who knew that I had a severe learning disability that affected my physical coordination, saw me lighting a candle while my hand was shaking. He said "Dave are you going to be a brain surgeon?" I laughed and I knew I could put it in perspective because I knew that he respected me. I guess the bottom line is, be willing and able to take gentle ribbing.

My fraternity brothers messed with me all of the time in a loving affectionate way. I knew that it was their way of showing that they respected and loved me, like a brother. It also challenged me to contrast it with what I was previously accustomed to. You can bet, there was an extreme polarization.

Getting playfully tormented by real friends, keeps you humble and it doesn't spoil you into getting your way all of the time, which is something we all learn eventually in life. If you are sensitive about some things, acknowledge and admit what they are and don't tease others about similar things that you know you have a hard time taking.

If you feel the need to confer with one who said something uncalled for, consult with that person in a civil, diplomatic manner by reasoning with him or her. When you have to disagree, don't take pride in being disagreeable (Martin and Osborne 391). This is difficult. I am guilty of it myself now and then.

No matter what, I believe that everyone, including little children, have the ability to distinguish between what is polite or rude, courteous or discourteous, and respectful or disrespectful.

Kids today, seem to be learning more and faster than ever because of the Information Age. Practitioners, who work with physically and mentally abused children, often tell them "If it doesn't feel right, it probably isn't." That same principle applies to adults who are unjustly criticized.

I guess above all, you must preach "The Golden Rule"- "Do unto others as you would have them do unto you." After all, you are a human being. You are also a special and unique individual and you must stay that way regardless of what someone else demands. Beware of that!

CHAPTER NINE

Individuality vs. Conformity

To Thine Self Be True

– William Shakespeare

You are a unique and special individual. It makes no difference what you do, especially if you are honest, trustworthy, decent, and you do what you know to be right for others and yourself. It makes no difference if you are a politician, farmer, coal miner, corporate executive, custodian, social worker, soldier, and so on. If you are meant to be any of those things, it is all the more rewarding when you are true to yourself: the unique individual.

I learned a technique from my Graduate School studies, entitled the "money concept." I was taught that no matter how someone mistreats you, or makes you feel stomped on, or rotten or mangled (a $20.00 bill is wrinkled, stomped on, and kicked around), you are still a worthy person, just as the money is (Jacobs 27).

What you hold valuable in yourself is what makes you feel special. As long as you can hold onto that belief, no one can take it away. If a $20 bill had a mind of it's own and realized it's own value based on the amount it is worth, it would still remain $20.00.

John Lennon had sung "We All Shine On." You need to shine on as an individual and continually flourish with your unique individuality, in a world endlessly composed of diversity.

There is such a rich mass of diversity in the human race, and some may claim that they appreciate it in every person, but believe me, they don't. Being different is no sin. In many respects, it is a gift.

Sadly, too often, we develop identities based on the views of others. Much of this is because no one wants to follow his/her path alone, because there is safety in numbers. However, adhering pathetically to the safety of the mores can be dangerous in the long run. You may not know what you are missing out on until it is too late. PARAMOUNT!

Schools claim that their curriculums are established to meet the individual needs for every student. Not all schools and teachers put those words into action. Quite often, there is no bridge between theory and practice.

Conformity in schools

In school, I was victimized by who did best, who was best, and who was more successful by conformity standards. I was not encouraged to express my identity and inner feelings or to embrace my musical and poetry interests. People hardly knew me. They did not know how unique my talents really were, partly, because I was obligated to conform.

In the music video, "Subdivisions" by the rock band Rush, the outcast is depicted as watching a Rush music video on television; his perturbed parents bitterly demand that he hit the books. This signifies the shallow, mainstream conventional standards, to do something without questioning authority: CONFORMITY (Price CS and Price RM 37).

Schools and all kinds of social situations demand conformity at the expense of one sacrificing his/her unique individuality. Schools demand that you earn the honor roll, be a superstar athlete, and attend all of the dances, especially the senior prom which in my opinion is the most overrated social event in life itself.

You don't have to do something just because everyone else is doing it (especially in a school structure). A senior prom is nothing more than a dance at the end of the school year. I went to mine and I had a decent time with my date, but I don't look back on it with fond memories. I went to the Pink Floyd concert at Three Rivers Stadium in Pittsburgh three nights after the prom. If the show was the same night as the prom, I would have gone to the concert instead. The Pink Floyd concert meant so much more to me than some cheesy, notoriously superficial social function.

I threw away my pictures from my prep school. I even gave away all of my yearbooks from the prep school (all seven of them). When any memories conjure up pain and emptiness instead of joy, I can exercise my individuality by being true to myself and doing what I know is best to make me feel content rather than conforming.

Things that appear to be conformity are not invariably so

If you engage in something that is definitely you, even if it is a fad and you have peace of mind, you are not conforming. I wore jams in high school because I liked them and I thought that I looked good in them. Sometimes being a part of a collective function may appear to be conformity but it is not necessarily so. For example, there was one bar in the community of the college that I attended that had numerous frequent patrons who congregated there regularly. I did not become a regular to necessarily go with the flow, even though it was the only place aside from the fraternity parties and the other housing units where people would socialize. I went there because I felt comfortable there and I honestly enjoyed it without feeling like I was conforming. It was some place that I personally loved to go to.

The appreciation of my college years has inspired me to attend reunions and other social functions because of who I am. However, I dread the idea of attending any social or recreational functions from my former prep school, especially class reunions. That would be like the NAACP insisting on holding a togetherness rally with the Ku Klux Klan. However, there are people that give in because of peer pressure.

Peer Pressure

Many people tend to go with the flow out of fear of being cast out. Some boys may not want to drink or smoke, but ubiquitous peer pressure may compel them to do so, just so they won't feel left out. Girls may feel pressured by their girlfriends or their female peers to do the same. More so, girls might feel obligated to compete with boys as to how much and how fast they consume alcohol, just to be more socially compatible and competent.

The peer pressure monster has profound clout and is hard to tame. In other words, it can be difficult to not give into it. There were times when I gave in to an extent.

The "Subdivisions" song from Rush conveys the message of how young people feel pressured to conform in high school environments and the homogenized outlets where teenagers shop: Malls. The same concept applies for the cellar taverns and the back seats of parked automobiles, because people feel the gravitational pull of peer pressure to drink alcohol, especially underage, and to have sex in the hot rod love shacks (Price CS and Price RM 36-38).

I remember a news commentator in my local area, saying that the area is so big on sports and it seemed to be the primary emphasis. He said that if an intercultural event of arts and music was brought into the area, it would not be as well received as a championship football game. He conceded that sports shouldn't be a bigger deal than other events since intercultural components are also significant, but sports were a big deal, so deal with it. Does that mean, conform or be like a worm?

A kid studying to be a musician or an artist attends a concert or event that is not the main thing that everyone else attends (local weekly summer dance); he/she should attend the dance without consideration of anything else, right? That seems to imply that it is fine to sacrifice your personal identity, because at least you will meet more people, hence know people better (not necessarily), and your chances of developing friendships with these people are better, even if your acceptance level is at best, superficial, peripheral, and marginal.

Basically the purported message is that the more you superficially interact with others, somehow, some way, you will be happy, no matter how much you alienate yourself from who you really are. No matter what, you will have inner peace as long as you conform to a social norm that is derived solely from outside influences regardless of how you feel on the inside. That theory is about as realistic and reasonable as staring into the sun to improve one's vision!!

I know from my experiences, observations, and conversations with others that many shallow ideologies can be dreadfully damaging on an emotional level.

No shame in being yourself

Some of us contrast our plight with others who are much more disadvantaged, and we feel guilty as a result. This is reasonable and understandable and it does help us put things in perspective. It also makes us more compassionate and understanding. Nevertheless, it does not invalidate any empty spaces that we truly need to have filled.

People are told they should not make waves, not even a ripple. That kind of conformist philosophy can be detrimental to one's spiritual growth. Certainly, no one likes to feel like a misfit (misused, ignored, or refused). Loneliness is very painful; I speak from experience. It is important to realize that we all need to be ourselves and feel as though we belong.

At all costs, you must be true to yourself. It is easy to follow the crowd, but eventually you come to realize that you are a unique person, who is special in his/her own way and you must maintain the integrity to keep it that way.

It is hard to defy peer pressure and other dimensions that demand conformity, but if you jump on the bandwagon every time, you could trap yourself into mazes that you have created which can spark a long-term malaise for you personally. If people are forced or feel forced, to be subjugated, then, they will follow blindly, like a flock of sheep when they don't say things, just to avoid being insulted or disliked; they are simply conforming.

The same concept applies when sensitive youths fight desperately to fit in by looking tough and getting in to fights. One may be recognized but still feel very lonely, because a profound hollowness may be pervading him. This is because his sensitivity is working against him on a long-term positive level. At any rate, once the youth is accepted, he will ironically feel dissatisfied and empty. You see; just because you're accepted doesn't mean you belong (Price CS and Price RM 105-06).

One could argue that being shallow is being congruent with one's nature and identity; therefore, that person is being an individual. Nevertheless, the individual cheats himself or herself out of growing to his/her spiritual maximum; this is due to the refusal of looking deeper. Despite our uniquenesses, we all have superficial tendencies. Everyone has them, but that is no excuse for being unwilling to look closer or think more deeply.

I remember being dismayed when some of my friends had done things that seemed to signify conformity. In retrospect, I realize that I was not being insightful or understanding enough of the other person because I was thinking more about myself. I was thinking in terms of accepting others the way that I wanted them to be rather than accepting them the way that they were. After all, they could have reprimanded me on faults that I had, the same way I could have done to them.

Mind you, I do not think it is okay for people to become alcohol abusers, be indiscriminately promiscuous, smoke tobacco or marijuana, or do anything they want just because their peers have more clout over them than anyone else. I drank beer in high school when I was 15, which was a stupid thing to do. Peer pressure may have contributed to an extent, but I was more than willing to engage in it.

I do not want to say that it is fine for a boy or a girl to get their bodies tattooed or pierced. Personally, I don't approve of any of that; I never did it myself and I would never encourage anyone to do it. Nevertheless, I think that it is wrong to demand that you conform to an uncompromisingly conventional status quo, without thinking for yourself. On the other hand, I think people who do those things are probably conforming, more than they are willing to admit.

Nevertheless, any trademarks from persons that seemingly buck the tide, may actually be expressions of their identities with pride. Who's to say? He or she may be honestly representing something as an authentic attribute of his/her identity rather than doing so because this is the new thing and everyone else is doing it. It doesn't necessarily mean that some-one is being emulated or does it?

Hero-worship and behaving in accordance with so-called role models and idols, without being yourself, is another sample of conformity. It is a way of seeking others to establish your values by making others more significant than you when you model their behaviors rather than estab-lishing your own values. Role models are people just like everyone else. They make mistakes and they have faults and weaknesses, no matter how much the media and the public amplify their popular images. They are not superior to you at all, contrary to the larger than life personas that they convey (Dyer 143-44). They know it themselves.

If you place people above you and strive to emulate them without acknowledging your own identity, you will plummet into the abyss of conformity. It is fine to borrow characteristics of persons that are char-ismatic to you and incorporate them into your personality to make you feel fulfilled and bolster your self-esteem. That is, as long as you truly perceive that as something that is reflective of you and you can honestly relate to it, and not do things just because you think others will think you are cool (143-44).

When <u>Miami Vice</u> was on television, boys and men wore clothing like Don Johnson's and left their faces unshaved because Don Johnson was popular. I construed this as conformity because people were trying to look hip, and the attempted emulation appeared to be preposterous, since it was so obvious as to who they were modeling. Know yourself as unique no matter how much you relate to others.

Being an avid fan of the 1970's cop show <u>Starsky & Hutch</u>, I learned to acknowledge myself as unique, even though I modeled and still do model some behaviors of David Soul's "Hutch" character, not because I rank him higher than myself but I saw things in his persona that I could see in myself. He was not just charismatic because he played a tough cop. I could see other things in him that seemed to mirror me, even though the reflections were limited and not fully precise. Since his char-acter and the character of his partner struck a chord with me, I could not help but model after them by thinking I am like them in some ways, but not exactly, especially "Hutch." I admired them and looked up to them but I perceived myself as being distinct from them. More than that, I have seen David Soul in other characters that he has played, which I was able to see a reflective part of myself.

You can consider the ideologies and attributes of charismatic persons to a point by conceding some validity to what they say. Still, you can de-velop your own theories based on thinking independently for yourself.

Alfred Adler was a protégé of Sigmund Freud who eventually became his rival when he pioneered his theory of social compensation, which was in contrast with Freud's psychoanalytical rhetoric (Corsini and Wedding 12-13). Plato was a student of Socrates but in time, Plato developed his own theories. They both had conflicting philosophical perspectives. Their intellectual minds stemmed from their unique individualities (Pojman 115).

Never make someone else's behavior more important than yours'

If you lean on people too much in a way that they become more significant than you, you conform and you enhance your own spiritual vegetation and atrophy. Measuring your own merit in contrast to others and becoming dissatisfied, immobilizes you from ascending as a unique individual. It is ludicrous to think of yourself as valuable based solely on outside opinions that may indeed be shallow. If you do, you are conforming rather than empowering yourself as a unique individual (Dyer 192).

Let's say that you are making a **movie of your life** and you want to look as though you are the star of the film, who is unique and special, but you have to view your life the way it is right now. If you feel like a slave to certain members of your family, then, you feel like a character who is secondary if not insignificant. You are seeing your life the way it is now and you realize that you are not behaving congruently with your true nature. If you give in to family members who make you feel compromised or subdued, you are allowing them to be the directors and producers of a film about the story of your life. Don't beat yourself up into thinking that your life is less important (Jacobs 100).

When you realize how good and special you are, you will be less concerned about what others think of you. If you are secure, you won't demand others to see things your way, or be just like you. You are unique (Dyer 70).

Trying to force others to do things your way, cheats them from growing as unique individuals. What you truly like in certain individuals is what makes them distinct and unique. The more self-love that you develop, the more freely you will be able to bless others with the love that they need to be who they really are. You must love yourself as a unique person before you can sufficiently love others.

You have an obligation to make yourself happy rather than making others happy. There is no need to feel any guilt for it. If you conform to the demanding happiness of others, you become enslaved to them and you will feel remorse only because they were merely thinking more of themselves rather than you. That is an unjust paradox for yourself that you should never succumb to (Dyer 207-08).

People become surprised when you stand your ground firmly based on your principles by saying "I believe in what I say, do, and think, and if you disapprove," "you'll have to deal with your own feelings about it" (Dyer 69-70). This "self-reliance" is very helpful (53, 59).

Confronting and challenging conflicts of interest will bolster your ability to be more efficient in handling anything and anyone that seems to threaten you. I know that it is difficult to be desensitized to the diatribe of a heckler or a detractor, but if you politely and diplomatically say, "okay, that is your opinion and you are entitled to it," you will feel more empowered when you respect the opinion of another by acknowledging his/her individuality (69-70).

Creating your own value system

Having your own personal value system is a golden dimension for anyone. You can do so by listing what you believe in and what you pretend to embrace. Create your own code of ethics based on your critical mind rather than what other people say. For example, I send out Christmas cards to friends and relatives whom I seldom see as opposed to relatives that I talk to periodically. I may say Happy Holidays to them on the telephone, but the Christmas card emphasis is exercised in my own way, because I think of myself as an individual who is doing what he truly desires. If I did otherwise, I would be conforming to outside values that threaten to compromise who I really am. You are unique and special and you must do what you can to remain that way. You've been that way from the day you were born.

God has created all of us to be unique and special, and this comes from our individualities. And since He loves us and wants us to love others, we can do that more effectively when we be ourselves in the most positive way.

Who and what you are: God's Creation of You: The unique and special individual that He has created. Part of God's plan for you: Letting yourself be who and what you are meant to be through thinking, acting, and behaving through your law of nature.

I use the phrase law of nature because I think God wants all of us to behave and flourish by being ourselves. This is a theory, of course. He wants us to fear Him yet love Him. His spirit speaks to us when we ponder as to what is best for ourselves and pray to Him.

God basically says that you should obey Him for the law that He makes, which instructs you to be who you are and do what you know is best for you. You do this more by exercising your freewill to make your personal choices and be who you are; this is how you preserve your unique individuality.

Anything and everything is unique. Environments are unique for each individual. Bethany College was and is, arguably, the most unique environment for me.

All animals are unique. It doesn't matter whether it is a rhinoceros or a butterfly. They are both organic specimens of matter, and they use energy whether it is kinetic or potential. Minute rocks and minerals may be inorganic samples of matter, but they are still unique based on being composed of molecules made up of atoms, which are made up of protons, neutrons, electrons, and positrons.

Energy is defined as the ability to do work and matter is defined as whatever takes up space. We should know that the different jobs and tasks that we engage in are unique, especially if you distinguish persons from different professions, such as lawyers, bankers, rust repairers, masons, teachers, doctors, musicians, football coaches, etc. (all samples of matter). Their active involvements in their occupations constitute energy, no matter how active or inactive they may appear to be on the surface.

There are so many unique elements that make us what we are, including all of the biological/chemical components of our anatomies and our genes, which are minute chromosomes that influence the inheritance and development of characteristics passed on by our parents.

The environment that we live in and all of the stressors in it influence and enhance our unique natures and so do our emotions. Therefore, everyone should be open to these ideas. Our central nervous systems, which are comprised of our brains, spinal cords, and all other neurons, are part of our unique identities.

Matter and energy are made up of so many different chemical elements. This includes the most microscopic particles of all, which we know are in every individual's brain. If these elements are unique and different in each unique individual's brain, which is used to help us think, learn, and comprehend, then how could our educational systems that have traditionally taught these scientific principles tell us that one learning system is appropriate for everyone? That is such a shattering tragic paradox.

We are taught that there is one uniform standard to learning and behaving, even when we are told that we are unique. Some people need to reexamine this contradiction because it doesn't make any sense. Nobody learns precisely the same way as anyone else. We think, learn, study and work differently based on our unique identities (Mooney and Cole 69).

I have adjusted to a learning style and I have accepted it. More than that, I can't change it. I can merely accept it and be the best that I can be. How can you put something in a certain place when it simply doesn't fit?

I do not fight a deficit in my brain, just a quintessential philosophy of conformity that is coldly demanded from the shallow opinions of others (Mooney and Cole 65).

Performance in school does not define what and who we are. It does not reveal how worthy we are as individuals either. Our identities are independent and more significant than our performance and successes.

Acknowledging the uniqueness of every individual should apply in any setting ranging from a casual, lighthearted conversation while having a beer, or to communicating as to how people can best get along when they are living together.

Since we are all merely human, an essential quality of one's humanity is that no one is perfect. Another significant factor is that everyone is a unique individual. We all do have limits and weaknesses, therefore we have no obligations to be mechanically efficient at all times like we are robots, contrary to what many others tell us.

CHAPTER TEN

More Theories of Individuality

When you rely on a consistent, linear, sequential structure, as though you are being programmed by some computer automation, it can be so drab and bleak, it can make you feel like a zombie, especially if you are deprived of using any of your unique skills and talents.

We've all heard that computers are only as intelligent as the people who program them. That is very true. Of course, they are not the living entities as we human beings are. In other words, if we allow ourselves to be programmed by authoritative others to be robots, then we are more prone to behave that way. Therefore, we are more likely to sacrifice being our true selves.

Robotics

Multisensory robots (computers that are structured to accomplish a multitude of tasks, and be compliant with their surroundings) are not yet operating as prevalently as people feared them to be. Fortunately, there is a great disenchantment and disapproval, not just by supplanted workers but society as a whole (Wallace and Hall 326-27).

Robotics and computers can undermine employment opportunities for both inexperienced and proficient workers. Robotics is viewed as management's way to keep everything in line economically - as robotics becomes more prevalent. Workers could be stripped away from their unique individualities as well as their humanities (327).

We are all evolutionists before we are revolutionists. In other words, we must develop as unique individuals and be true to our human natures, before any potential compliance to innovative standards in society that threaten to own us. This concept is denoted in the classic film Our Man Flint (The United States answer to James Bond 007), starring the late James Coburn. The world is about to be controlled by mad scientists who have created an earthquake machine and women are changed into robots. They are transformed (perhaps hypnotically) into "pleasure units" for men - as though they are prostitution slaves.

The original <u>Stepford Wives</u>, starring Katharine Ross is relative to <u>Our Man Flint</u>, which conveys the ultimate of every male chauvinist's dream. As we know, these concepts are allegorical of the way women are degraded and mistreated in society. They are often burglarized of their uniqueness because they are indoctrinated into thinking that being homemakers, wives, and mothers are what solely make them who and what they are.

There is no absolute individual nature that would accurately describe all human beings, regardless of gender. When people believe that there is, their lives become bleak and insipid when they behave like androids, especially when they don't go beyond their constrictive realms that make them feel secure (Price CS and Price RM 22).

We have tendencies to avoid things because we fear changes when we are so acclimated to our safety net areas. This is especially so, when we feel forced to make changes in our lives to help others whom we normally may not wish to be in direct contact with.

However, when we come to realize that everyone is human and a unique individual, we feel challenged to help each person become such, not just so they can live in peace with the rest of us, but so they can live peacefully with themselves; this becomes a grim reminder to you, the unique individual to be yourself. You become aware, that it is so critical for everyone to evolve from one's self-formation plan rather than being embroiled in some "aggregate sector of conformity." This concept is derived from a phrase from the Rush song, "Subdivisions," written by drummer and lyricist, Neil Peart and sung by Geddy Lee. Being true to one's nature helps you be independent of the "Aggregate Sectors of Conformity" (Price CS and Price RM 34-40).

Our psychic drives are simple and uncontaminated, but they are sometimes obstructed due to outside barriers. The stakes are always high and the risks keep looming larger when one declares ownership of his/her identity. It is very difficult to stem the evil tide amid a sea of conformity. However, it is crucial to maintain your identity, and if you can honestly do so, without having any regrets for not doing things demanded by others, then you can feel fulfilled regardless of what they think (Price CS and Price RM 109). Besides wasting personal talents, it will be more difficult to know and find yourself when you are immersed in the first two "aggregate sectors of conformity" (Price CS and Price RM 34-40).

"There are three things extremely hard, steel, a diamond, and to know oneself" - Benjamin Franklin (Myers 38).

God only knows how long it takes for each individual to know himself or herself, and where he/she belongs. Familiar and even intimate persons in your life can indeed be strangers when they know nothing about your uniqueness, thus, they may know nothing about you at all.

One thing is for sure, we are misled into believing that collective institutions are greater than the specific individuals who comprise them. There is no real exclusive life if you don't struggle to know yourself as an individual. You very well could remain in an "aggregate sector of conformity" (Price CS and Price RM 34-40).

The first sector of the "Aggregate Sectors of Conformity" comes from an area that we are all familiar with; it represents suburbia. Suburban neighborhoods generally appear to be structured geometrically. They are emphasized as buffer zones between the urban neon life, made up of crime and too much of a fast pace, and the ideologies of each human being preserving his/her uniqueness, no matter where they are and what they do with what they have (34-40).

The Monkees song, "Pleasant Valley Sunday" is a subtle, aural portrait of youth breaking free from the suburban mainstream, because the youngsters are disenchanted and exasperated with the stale dullness. Of course, it takes time for the children to grow up before they begin to see things realistically because they go through those years where life appears to be so beautiful and wonderful. Often times, persons in mainstream conventional neighborhoods, cannot flourish in any realms of boredom. They inevitably seek something more colorful and exciting (36).

Urban life and life in the fast lane of singles bars, dance clubs, and the like, represent the second sector of the "Aggregate Sectors of Conformity." Cities may be composed of pandemonium, but there is creativity that spawns from the intercultural disharmony, because the diversity is ever so conspicuous. Of course, urban nightlife is generally perceived from a deeper perspective to be spiritually bankrupt, because you see every social facet of life, which is really nothing at all. This is particularly so, if your primary and habitual goals are meeting with people on short-term levels to mindlessly get laid, drunk, or stoned. People become part of a social norm in the urbanite vicinities by dressing in specific fashions that ironically are like prep school monkey suits. Many continually strive to be a part of it (37-39).

People cash in their dreams for what is nothing more than short-term lust, but they don't learn it until much later, because they are rushing (and in some cases, headlong) for instant action and pleasure. Of course, some runaways who have rebelled against the suburban pack, become prostitutes to reinforce their drug habits, or people survive by pushing drugs. The more people look out for number one, the more they shaft others along the way (39).

Either way, if people are successful or unsuccessful by just trying to fit in, without being truly honest and content with themselves, they conform to being members of an idle lifestyle devoid of rich vigor and uniqueness, no matter how colorful it may appear on the surface (34-40).

Eventually, the third sector becomes engendered when the authentic self breaks free from the brainwashing traps of the suburban and urban aggregate sectors of conformity. It can be hard to break free from the first two sectors. It can be hard to find a healthy balance between the two (39-40).

Eventually, the loner finds that new beliefs can obliterate old friendships that were shallow and pretentious (Price CS and Price RM 109). You then have new aspirations to find and cultivate new friends. This leads to the 3rd dimension: Looking for and finding yourself, and growing from that point on (39-40).

The third sector of the "Aggregate Sectors of Conformity" connotes that we must look inward for direction and to chart our educational and spiritual paths. Assimilating ideas on a homogenous level fails to recognize that our minds are wired differently. There is no shame in expressing yourself on a nonverbal level, particularly if that is how you best communicate with others on an intellectual plane.

It is paramount that you lead a life less ordinary and more innovative for you personally. I don't want to be normal in the sense that I seem like a robot. This self-reflection is vital for the development of one's self-formation plan, as opposed to looking outward for acceptance (34-40).

Behaving robotically doesn't get you anywhere spiritually if you are displaced from an area where you should be: **A FISH OUT OF WATER!!!** You all must remain perpetually proactive with your own skills and being true to yourself: the unique individual.

What may be an interesting paradox is that leaders in all dimensions who demand social conformity do not think they are stringing people along in the wrong paths as individuals. This is based on fear of losing control and being overpowered for whatever reasons. As a result, they demand conformity based on a status quo. However, they may have unknowingly renounced their obligations to be themselves on a true, inspirational level. Therefore, they choose a linear structure, and they demand that others conform to that structure, no matter how dark and hollow it may be (Price CS and Price RM 68).

Being so profoundly sheltered and isolated, I realized later that I was living in a dark dungeon. I was misled into thinking that there were only certain things in this life that really counted and those were the cultural ideas and events that I experienced. I was not inspired to broaden my horizons whatsoever and I realized how limited and narrow my world was later on and suffered the consequences.

Of course, a turning point culminated when I knew that I had to learn so much more about life when realizing that life had so much more to offer.

Once I ascended into a higher, brighter and expansive world, I was enthralled to see a world that was so illuminatingly photogenic. I also saw a stark contrast from a world that was so shallow and vapid.

I must admit I had felt uncomfortable at times with making changes in my life from what I was previously accustomed to. I still feel this way now more than ever despite the optimism and inspiration. I really felt pain, anger, sorrow, and guilt because I became more tragically aware of what I missed out on. However, I am confident that I will get used to the changes and cherish them as I have done so already. That is why I am trying to inspire all of you out of the prison cells that you have been locked into.

I see the glistening dimension of truth and I feel compelled to lead the masses to it so you can all think freely for yourselves as individuals. However, if I were to force these notions on you, I would be falling into the evils of imposing conformity, which would be an impasse for each individual dweller. If individuals do not create their own paths, they merely survive and they are content to be robots for a collective order. This is very relative to <u>The Republic</u> authored by Plato (Heisenberg 76-77).

Rush: 2112

Neil Peart of Rush, has written songs that primarily regard being motivated to find and retain your unique identity, reach your goals, and to establish a brighter vision of the future for you personally (Price CS and Price RM back flap synopsis). 2112, an album and rock opera by Rush issued in 1976, is a story about a future space era renegade who becomes a revolutionary, with music as a vehicle for the freedom of individual expression (Swenson 3).

It all starts when the protagonist discovers a unique musical instrument that is spiritually uplifting and liberating for him personally. It is introduced to the priests who govern the "New World Order" on a seemingly communist level. They provide music on a linear Muzak, saying this is what is needed to keep the world politically and economically balanced. This proves to be nothing more than spiritually lackluster for the individual over time. He eventually becomes a renegade after the priests reject his presentation of the strange yet arguably inspiring sample of music that he has created.

The protagonist maintains this source of music, not just to denote the concept of enjoying the music that suits you personally, but to exercise your freedom of expression regardless of what any "aggregate sector of conformity" coldly demands. This not only applies in this particular story, but in every aspect of life, as we know it.

The 2112 story signifies "that every single facet of every life is regulated and directed" by the priests, including the "newspapers," "books," "music," and the "work" that is done. Basically the main character finds some instrument and he "produces" his "first harmonious sounds," which become his "own music." One priest declaims the music as something that will ruin the future; therefore, it is unacceptable.

The leaders of the "Brotherhood of Man" under the "Red Star of the Solar Federation" demand efficiency on a collective plane. The protagonist then realizes that he must go beyond the perimeters of the communist establishment, and be in alliance with his self-formation plan. He was told just like many in society that he must conform and remain factitious.

The rebel leads an innovative uprising of individuality through music. One of the most significant messages in the story connotes that personal integrity and artistic integrity are intimately related. You can use one as a symbol for the other (Price CS and Price RM 93).

"Something For Nothing," represents the finality of the story, and it is arguably the most pivotal song of the 2112 opera. The final set of lyrics, implies that you will eventually rule your own kingdom by owning and being yourself, when you follow your heart and think with your head.

Your mission in life is to blossom forth into your unique person-hood: Yourself. Herman Hesse's classic Siddhartha, is about a young man in India during the era of Gotama Buddha. He goes on a trek for identity and enlightenment, which is akin to the Buddha's odyssey (10-19). The Buddha was a revolutionary, who disregarded norms and the same paths that were taken by the same people (20-29). Siddhartha learns from the Buddha, to not take the same path. He merely establishes his own (90).

The real individualist does not establish norms for others. He urges individuals to think for themselves based on being unique individuals.

When you remain an individual, you may not have friends on all levels. Your true friends will understand that you must do whatever it takes to help you personally glisten, and they will remain your friends since they are following their hearts and keeping their personal dreams alive. One grows when he/she refines his/her talents, even though there is a limit to how far you can elongate yourself. No matter what, you are somebody, so you must do what you think is right based on you being the independent, intelligent individual rather than blindly following someone else. Exercise your will to be yourself (Price CS and Price RM 112).

No matter how difficult and lonely your life may be, you must do everything in your power to preserve your unique individuality, no matter what the cost is and the sacrifices that go along with it. You simply cannot give up, no matter how tough it gets, and if you give in or give up, it only gets horrendously worse; take it from me. In the movie, Tecumseh: The Last Warrior, the Shawnee Indian warrior says "Surrender Is Not Peace."

The Who's Tommy - The Individual

Tommy, from The Who's rock opera of the same name, is a unique individual. I can identify with Tommy in some ways. Tommy was a happy, wholesome child just like I was, until he suffers a trauma that makes him emotionally and spiritually handicapped. He is not necessarily "deaf," "dumb," or "blind" on a physical level; he just appears to be catatonic. In fact, a pivotal lyric in the story comes when a specialist examines him, and he states that he hears, but he is too walled in to respond to anyone. This denotes how post-traumatic-stress-disorder victims are so ultimately immersed in their painful memories and flashbacks, they isolate themselves into a particular emotional realm, and they seem unable to communicate with others even if they can actually see, hear, and maybe even speak.

An example of Tommy's plight would be from one of the "Dirty Harry" movies, Sudden Impact, starring Clint Eastwood. A vigilante woman seeks retribution against criminals who raped her and her sister. Her sister has sustained a profound case of PTSD. She is practically a vegetable. She is not the least bit verbally responsive. However, when the older sister tells her how she killed the first of many of who were responsible for the heinous crimes, the younger one sheds some tears. She could hear, but she just could not answer to whatever her sister says, because the trauma chronically stifles her.

Tommy's condition, along with the way he is mistreated, enhance him to isolate himself into a cocoon, so to speak. This enhances his social alienation from others. Tommy becomes more and more mistreated, which becomes emotionally damaging to him.

The same thing happened to me, only in a different way and not to the worst extreme. In my case, the impasse was there mainly because I was forced to dwell in a world that did not fit my individual needs. Worse than that, I hardly had anyone who listened to me nor even tried to understand me. I knew that there were people out there who had the compassion, understanding, and empathy in their hearts to accept me, love me, and help me be the best that I could be, but I did not know who or where they were and where they would be in the future. These were barriers, because there was an absence of resources. I am trying to be who and what I am in the world: This is all part of the ongoing quest for identity, which is a major concept of the Tommy story (Giuliano 86).

Tommy's ongoing yet vegetative stance through looking in the mirror signifies that he is trying to understand who he is by trying to find himself. He hopes that once he does, he will finally be at peace with himself, and be able to share and receive love from others, and be overjoyed with endless happiness. Everyone shares these thoughts.

Within the unique individual, there is a driving force that motivates one to go forward and beyond. I call this the "internal music note," which is derived from another attempted rock opera from Pete Townshend and The Who entitled Lifehouse. Tommy has this internal note as well and the more he retreats into his entranced state, the more he becomes in touch with it, even though he is not aware of it.

Music is composed of vibrations as matter and energy are. Tommy is a sample of matter and any work that he does is energy, whether it is kinetic or potential. He remains alive by following his heart through the guiding force of an internal music note, composed of vibrations. This is a driving force to help him live and transcend at some point (Giuliano 84-85).

Perhaps the underlying message is no matter how deprived, neglected, forsaken, and miserable that you are during some periods in your lives, you must retain your spirit and identity the best way that you can. More than that, you must search for and establish values that help you maintain your integrity. What's ironic, is that the more spiritually bankrupt that you feel, the more determined you will be to replenish that emptiness, by using that motivating force that is in all of us. This is the "internal music note," which enables you to roll with the punches. We are all like flowers that need to blossom with the right resources to help us grow but we need our internal urges to motivate us. Helen Keller must have had that same note too, and she was physically deaf, dumb, and blind.

At any rate, the music of <u>Tommy</u> is a message to the listener that we become aware of his existence and plight by the discerning vibrations that he feels on the inside. This enhances the music note that keeps him moving forward, as vague and limited as that may be in his lethargic state (Giuliano 85).

I believe all of the music notes are derived from the deeply rooted thoughts and feelings of the author himself: Pete Townshend. He was a pariah of the worst kind. He was taunted, alienated, and felt unknown and unloved. The subtle, internal vibrations in Tommy (his inner thoughts and feelings) lead me to infer that those were the same ones that Townshend had. These vibrations helped generate the inner drive of Townshend. As a result, he expressed them through the lyrics and music of <u>Tommy</u> (84-85).

I can relate to Tommy because my estrangement from others compelled me to follow my heart and do everything that I could to remain the unique individual that I was. I was following the music note inside me that would keep me humming along. This instructed me to be true to myself and do well with what I had, where I was. In a way, I did this during the most turbulent period of my life.

Townshend explored himself the same way that I did, and we were both fortunate enough to enjoy music, which substantiated the internal drives in both of us. I have always cherished the music of The Who and many of the other bands that I listened to from <u>102.5 WDVE</u>, an AOR station in Pittsburgh that I was a hardcore listener of.

Listening to music and lyrics enhances me to appreciate and learn about life. I think that a person's appreciation of any genre of music conveys distinct characteristics of any unique person. Moreover, the more that you truly appreciate those specific music genres, the more that you will be inspired to be the unique individuals that you really are. I think that my love for music implies special and unique qualities in my self. Being so rabidly passionate of the music I love is an authentic reflector of my identity. It infused me with pride to maintain my individual integrity and say to hell with those insecure idiots who told me to conform to the music that they loved because that was most widely known and popular.

Music was a good coping resource, and if I didn't have it, I could have been in mental limbo then, and maybe even now. Music represented the route to revival for me, to give me a future with hope and vigor. In fact, this route led to one eventful night on the 10th of April in 1989. This pinnacle moment changed my life forever and made me feel revitalized and born again!!

April 10, 1989/
Conclusion

I started pledging Sigma Nu Fraternity during the second semester of my freshman year at Bethany. I realized as pledging went on that I was in dire need of making some new real friends, not just because I wanted to have more of a social life, but because I wanted to feel needed and loved as a unique individual, as well as a brother of the house. I really liked the active brothers of the house, and I was beginning to like my pledge brothers more and more, as I was getting to know them through pledging. I was earning respect little by little because everyone liked me for who I was. However, they still did not know me very well yet, and I felt more and more compelled for them to get to know me better.

I thought to myself that I would find brotherly love in my life if I share something with them about myself that is unique and special. If I continue to win and earn their love slowly, I will be able to love them and others more, as well as myself. Anyway, we pledges threw a party for the actives one night. Before and during this party, I was socializing with many of the brothers about rock & roll music. Later on, I was singing some Who songs with a few of the brothers. Some people were slowly getting to know me better through this unique aspect of my personality.

Over three weeks later, we had begun the anxiously but not pleasantly awaited Hellweek. It was tough to bear in the beginning, and I feared that I would lose control of trying to budget my time with everything I had to do. I basically feared that I was not going to make it through the week and then I would not be activated. I spoke to one of the actives who I knew from the beginning of the school year. He told me not to worry and that I would make it through and that I was going to have a great time that night. Then he asked me if I knew the words to the song, "Pinball Wizard" by The Who. I said yes and he said "good." I knew from that point on that something great was going to happen that night. I was getting excited.

We went back to the house and we went down to the basement to await the festivities. We were going to do an air band contest. The active brothers gave a demonstration of one. Then each pledge had to get in groups of fives based on how we counted off.

Shortly after the first group of pledges performed, my group was called into the backroom. I was told that we were going to perform "Pinball Wizard." Nobody knew the words to it but me; I was to sing it. I knew right there and then, that this was my chance to really exemplify my identity in a way that no one had ever seen before. I had been wanting to do this for a long time, not just to express myself but to receive love by giving love in a sense.

The music started nice and slow leading to the first verse. I started singing the first verse and strutting around the room in a very passion-ate, dogmatic, energetic way, like I was trying to emulate Roger Daltrey, the vocalist of The Who. My physical dynamics did not measure up to Daltrey's standards, but my passionate love of The Who's music was extremely obvious.

I remember seeing two of the active brothers turn to each other look-ing in awe after I had done the first verse. Then I just continued to sing and go through the physical motions all of the way through the entire song. There was a screaming explosion of adulation after the song had ended! God only knows what the decibel level was! This highpoint changed my life forever in a most positive way. I was getting high fives, handshakes, and hugs from all of the brothers. I knew more than ever that I found love in the form of brotherhood by attempting to give and share love as well as a part of my personality. I was more loved and ac-cepted than I had ever been in my life, and I was able to love them back. It has benefited me from that point on and we are like brothers to this day. Cheers!!

I had really shared something with them more than just my apprecia-tion of the music that I love which is an integral part of my unique per-sonality. It was my way of connecting with people on a heart-to-heart level to inspire the giving and receiving of love. Music definitely inspires that.

In retrospect, I know from this experience, that looking for love by truly giving love is the only way you will actually find love. Longing for love through hate is ineffective and terribly wrong. I will admit there is a part of me that wishes all of my detractors and anyone who thought that I was inferior from my past, would have been there to witness that glorious event, only they would have been out in the distance away from the people who were applauding me. This would not have been to just tell them off with a verb and a pronoun. More rightfully, it would have been a way to let them know that there are great, cool, unique, charismatic, special people in the world who think that I am cool and special and they respect and love me for it.

It doesn't matter what others think, especially when I am surrounded by these special people as often as I can be. They love me and they help me shine on, and when you keep shining on, you will discover that what you really need is love.

Of course, it is pretty hard to shine on as a unique individual not to mention a human being if you don't have anyone to share your successes with and you are too lonely and isolated to have anyone around you who will enhance you with the courage and strength that you need to flourish and transcend. You merely remain empty hearted if you are unable to give or receive love if you don't have a real family, real love, or real friends that encourage you to hold your head up and never give up. That's not to say that you won't succeed in life if you lack these "human resources" so to speak, it is just that you will feel much more like a winner, if you have people to share your successes with as well as your life. This is just food for thought because every unique individual needs other unique individuals.

I was dreadfully cheated out of a beautiful opportunity to have an enriching education inside and outside of the classroom before I attended Bethany College. A school experience that could have and should have been filled with a happy, wholesome academic and social foundation. An era filled with an exposure to intercultural ideas, experiences on a social level with girls and making real friends, being taught to learn how to learn, and living life to the fullest rather than being a vegetable who really seemed to have missed the boat on life. If I had the opportunity and freedom to make mistakes during those years between the 8th grade and my senior year in high school, I would have learned from them, and not made as many mistakes later on. Of course, as long as I am still alive, my life will go on and I plan to take it to the maximum level and beyond. I have always been so fiercely compelled to compensate for way too many empty spaces in my life derived from an empty past and though progress has been made through the years, I still have a great deal to make up for.

Obviously, I can't change anything about my past, but I can use it to channel it in a positive way so your kids never have to go through what I had gone through. Those school years are extremely delicate and precious, and if you were denied a chance to live it and grow fruitfully with your peers, you would be astounded as to how it will haunt you ten to twenty years down the road after you finish high school. Any parents who are reading this - please don't take it for granted, because the psychological problems that your kids could have when they grow up will astonish you and those wounds are generally more difficult to endure than any physical wounds they may sustain. And of course, the consequences could be disastrous later on if they don't get the professional help that they would need before they have their own families.

What we are dealing with here is life. It is my life and it is your life. We are meant to evolve and flourish, not devolve and stagnate. Before you get into the final section of the book which informs you about my sequentially produced ideas for the future based on the second book to be published, I will leave you with a poem that sums up the points of each chapter that you have read. Please take it to heart.

Just because I was born with something I can't change

based on how a few wires in my brain seemed to be crossed

does not make me any more or less strange

nor make my future hopes and dreams totally lost

as you know, I was put in a place where I didn't belong

this made me nothing more than a fish out of water

and though I did everything in my power to be strong

those seven years in school didn't get any hotter

but that doesn't mean that there was no chance of survival

because after high school, I entered a brand new world

and I knew there and then it was an era of revival

especially, since I was finally in a school that actually had girls

in college, you have an opportunity to grow with an open mind

this makes education and learning, very, very wholesome

but if you choose to be ignorant, you will eventually find

that being shallow will make your life, very, very fulsome

Being yourself with an open mind, can really enrich your life

this helps you show a positive attitude in a most cheerful fashion

this better enables you to use empathy and understanding

which makes you stronger and wiser with sympathy & compassion

You then learn to treat others with courtesy and respect

it makes no difference, whether or not someone has a defect

this is easily understood by even the worst kind of fool

which is all of the more reason to preach the golden rule

You must be true to your individuality, no matter what the cost

many opportunities could be blown away and tossed

if you sacrifice your identity, by complying with a narrow norm

just like robots that are programmed to constantly conform

sharing special moments with friends are things that we treasure

all of these things bring us together in good spirits and cheer

the love of our happy days is something you could never measure

especially whenever we have reunions drinking our favorite beer

no matter what, every human being is made of flesh and blood and

every individual is special and unique

and the more that you allow yourself to grow and bud

the more that you will reach your individual peak

Peace, love, and happiness God Bless!!

BE UNIQUE BE YOU AND LIVE

Works Cited

Albee, Edward. Commencement Address. Bethany College
  Commencement. Bethany, WV. 23 May 1992.

Axelson, John A. Counseling and Development in a Multicultural
  Society. Manuscript Ed. Lorraine Anderson. 2nd ed. Belmont:
  Brooks/Cole, 1993.

Cawood, D. Assertiveness for Managers: Learning Effective Skills
  for Managing People. 3rd ed. Bellingham: Intl. Self-Counsel, 1992.

Corsini, Raymond J., and Danny Wedding. Current Psychotherapies.
  5th ed. Itasca: F.E. Peacock, 1995.

Costner, Kevin, dir. Dances with Wolves. Perf. Costner, Tig, 1990.

Deutsch, A.R. How to Hold Your Job: Gaining Skills and Becoming
  Promotable in Difficult Times. Englewood Cliffs: Prentice, 1984.

Dolenz, Micky, David Jones, Michael Nesmith, and Peter Tork, perf.
  "Pleasant Valley Sunday." Writ. Carole King and Gerry Goffin.
  The Monkees Pisces, Aquarius, Capricorn, and Jones. Colgems,
  1967.

Duncan, Barry L. and Joseph W. Rock. "Saving Relationships: The
  Power of the Unpredictable." Psychology Today. Jan.-Feb. 1993:
  46+

Dyer, Wayne W. <u>Your Erroneous Zones: Step by Step Advice for Escaping the Trap of Negative Thinking and Taking Control of Your Life</u>. New York: Harper, 1976.

Eastwood, Clint, dir. <u>Sudden Impact</u>. Perf. Eastwood, Sondra Locke, and Pat Hingle. Warner Bros., 1983.

Elikann, Larry, dir. <u>Tecumseh: The Last Warrior</u>. Perf. Jesse Borrego. Turner, 1995.

Ellis, David B. <u>Becoming a Master Student: Tools, Techniques, Hints, Ideas, Illustrations, Instructions, Examples, Methods, Procedures, Processes, Skills, Resources and Suggestions for Success</u>. 5th ed. Rapid City: College Survival, 1985.

Forbes, Bryan, dir. <u>The Stepford Wives</u>. Perf. Katharine Ross. Palomar, 1975.

Giannetti, Louis. <u>Understanding Movies</u>. Prod. Ed. F. Hubert. 5th ed. Englewood Cliffs: Prentice, 1990.

Giuliano, Geoffrey. <u>Behind Blue Eyes: The Life of Pete Townshend</u>. New York: Plume, 1996.

Gordon, Sol. <u>Why Love is Not Enough [...]</u>. Boston: Bob Adams, 1988.

Heisenberg, Weiner. <u>Physics and Philosophy: The Revolution in Modern Science</u>. 2nd ed. New York: Harper, 1962.

Hesse, Hermann. <u>Siddhartha</u>. Trans. Hilda Rosner. New York: New Directions, 1951.

Huggins, Roy, and Jo Swerling Jr., prod. <u>Baretta</u>. Perf. Robert Blake, Michael D. Roberts, Ed Grover, and Tom Ewell. Universal. ABC. 1975-1978.

—. <u>Toma</u>. Perf. Tony Musante and Susan Strasberg. Universal. ABC. 1973-1974.

Jacobs, Ed. <u>Creative Counseling Techniques: An Illustrated Guide</u>. Odessa: Psychological Assessment Resources, 1992.

Jones, Cliff. <u>Another Brick in the Wall: The Stories Behind Every Pink Floyd Song</u>. London: Carlton, 1996.

Lee, Geddy, Alex Lifeson, and Neil Peart, perf. <u>Rush Chronicles</u>. Executive prod. Annette Cirillo. Videocassette. Anthem Polygram. 1990.

Lennon, John. "Instant Karma (We All Shine On)." Apple, 1970.

Lyman, Howard B. <u>Test Scores and What They Mean</u>. 5th ed. Needham Heights: Allyn, 1991.

Mann, Daniel, dir. <u>Our Man Flint</u>. Perf. James Coburn. 20th Century Fox, 1966.

Mann, Michael, and George Geiger, Executive prod. <u>Miami Vice</u>. Perf. Don Johnson, Phillip Michael Thomas, and Edward James Olmos. Universal. NBC. 1984-1989.

Martin, Garry L., and J. Grayson Obsorne. Psychology, Adjustment, and Everyday Living. Ed. Joan E. Foley. Acquisitions Ed. Susan Finnemore Brennan. Assistant Ed. Jennie Katsaros. 2nd ed. Englewood Cliffs: Prentice, 1993.

Martin, Quinn, prod. The Streets of San Francisco. Perf. Karl Malden and Michael Douglas. Warner Bros. ABC. 1972-1977.

McAdams, James, prod. Kojak. Perf. Telly Savalas, Dan Frazer, Kevin Dobson, and George Savalas. Universal. CBS. 1973-1978.

Mooney, Jonathan, and David Cole. Learning Outside the Lines: Two Ivy League Students with Learning Disabilities and ADHD Give You the Tools for Academic Success and Educational Revolution. New York: Fireside, 2000.

Myers, D.G. Social Psychology. Ed. Jeannine Ciliotta, Christopher Rogers, and James R. Belser. 4th ed. New York: McGraw, 1993.

O'Connor, Joseph, and John Seymour. Introducing Neuro-Linguistic Programming: Psychological Skills for Understanding and Influencing People. Rev. ed. San Francisco: Aquarian, 1993.

Parker, Alan, dir. Pink Floyd The Wall. Perf. Bob Geldof. MGM, 1982.

Peart, Neil, Geddy Lee, and Alex Lifeson, perf. Rush 2112. Prod. Peart, Lee, Lifeson, and Terry Brown. Mercury, 1976.

Peart, Neil, Geddy Lee, and Alex Lifeson. "Something for Nothing." Rush 2112. Mercury, 1976.

—. "Subdivisions." Rush Signals. Mercury, 1982.

Pojman, Louis P. Ethics: Discovering Right and Wrong. Belmont: Wadsworth, 1990.

Price, Carol Selby, and Robert M. Price. Mystic Rhythms: The Philosophical Vision of Rush. Berkeley Heights: Wildside, 1998.

Quinlan, Carol. "The Positives of ADHD." AOL Parenting. 20 Aug. 2001. <http://families.aol.momsonline.oxygen.com/ages and stages/education...article.asp? key = adhd022>.

Rogers, Carl. A Way of Being: The Latest Thinking on a Person-Centered Approach to Life by the Author of "On Becoming a Person." Boston: Houghton, 1980.

Russell, Ken, dir. Tommy. Perf. Ann-Margret, Oliver Reed, and Roger Daltrey. RSO, 1975.

Shaw, Tommy. "Styx Song Synopsis." Tape Delayed New Orleans Styx Concert. AOR Radio. WDVE, Pittsburgh. 15 July 1983.

Shaw, Tommy, Dennis DeYoung, James Young, Chuck Panozzo, and John Panozzo. "Fooling Yourself (The Angry Young Man)." Styx The Grand Illusion. A & M, 1977.

Spelling, Aaron, and Leonard Goldberg, prod. Charlie's Angels. Perf. Kate Jackson, Farrah Fawcett, Jaclyn Smith, Cheryl Ladd, David Doyle, and John Forsythe. Columbia. ABC. 1976-1981.

—. Starsky & Hutch. Perf. David Soul, Paul Michael Glaser, Antonio Fargas, and Bernie Hamilton. Columbia. ABC. 1975-1979.

Stargell, Willie, and Tom Bird. <u>Willie Stargell: An Autobiography</u>.
New York: Harper, 1984.

Sting. "Russians." <u>The Dream of the Blue Turtles</u>. A & M, 1985.

Swenson, John. Liner Notes. <u>Rush Chronicles</u>. Audiocassette. Mercury,
1990.

—. Liner Notes. <u>The Who By Numbers</u>. CD. MCA, orig. rel. 1975.
Exclusive CD rel. 1996.

Thomas, Danny, and Aaron Spelling, prod. <u>The Mod Squad</u>. Perf. Michael
Cole, Clarence Williams III, Peggy Lipton, and Tige Andrews.
World Vision. ABC. 1968-1973.

Thorndike, E.L., and Clarence L. Barnhart. <u>Thorndike Barnhart
Advanced Dictionary</u>. 2nd ed. Glenview: Scott, 1974.

Toma, David, and Irv Levey. <u>Toma Tells It Straight With Love: Wake Up
America! The Drug Epidemic is Destroying Us All</u>. New York:
JAN, 1981.

Townshend, Pete, Roger Daltrey, John Entwistle, and Keith Moon, perf.
<u>The Who Tommy</u>. Prod. Kit Lambert and Chris Stamp. MCA, 1969.

Townshend, Pete, Roger Daltrey, John Entwistle, and Keith Moon.
"In a Hand or a Face." <u>The Who By Numbers</u>. MCA, 1975.

—. "Pinball Wizard." Rec. 7 Feb. 1969. <u>The Who Tommy</u>. MCA, 1969.

Wallace, William A., and Donald L. Hall. Psychological Consultation: Perspectives and Applications. Pacific Grove: Brooks/Cole, 1996.

Waters, Roger, David Gilmour, Rick Wright, and Nick Mason, perf. Pink Floyd The Wall. Prod. Waters, Gilmour, and Bob Ezrin. Columbia, 1979.

Waters, Roger, David Gilmour, Rick Wright, and Nick Mason. "Another Brick in the Wall (Part 2)." Pink Floyd The Wall. Columbia, 1979.

Welles, Orson, dir. Citizen Kane. Perf. Welles, Joseph Cotten, and Agnes Moorehead. RKO, 1941.

Winkler, Henry. The Phil Donahue Show. Multi Media Entertainment. NBC. 16 Dec. 1988.

Index

It is time to accept unique individual persons for who and what they are instead of accepting them the way you want them to be!!

In this life, your parents, teachers, schools, and peers tell you that you must be something according to their terms and standards. If you sacrifice the real you in the process, tough!! It makes no difference whether or not you are truly happy as long as someone else is satisfied. That's all that really counts. You are being victimized by ignorance. Maybe you're some place where you don't belong. Maybe someone is trying to change you into something that you can't possibly be. They don't want the real you, they want a robot that they can program to conform to their narrow norm.

Be Unique Be You and Live is written by a loner – a man with a misdiagnosed, extraordinarily profound learning disability with ADD and an undiagnosed case of chronic depression for over half of his life. Being denounced as lazy, inferior and so forth, sustaining massive psychological damage, David A. George explicitly tells you his story about the nature of his learning disability and being at the mercy of a brutal school system during the most turbulent years of his life making him nothing but "A Fish Out of Water." David A. George astutely reminds you that you are a human being with basic and specific needs and he teaches you why you must be true to yourself and maintain your individual integrity at all costs, no matter what the odds against you are from anyone that demands conformity. Be Unique Be You and Live teaches you why you must be inspired to grow fruitfully and be your true real self. It also teaches why we should inspire all unique individuals to be their real selves so they can grow into well-rounded persons.

David A. George was a struggling student who succeeded later in school while attending Bethany College in West Virginia graduating with a GPA in the B range and succeeding in Graduate School earning a 3.8 GPA.

ISBN 0-9769970-0-2

$12.00 (U.S.)